BROKEN
PROMISES

BROKEN PROMISES

LIEUTENANT COLONEL TED BLICKWEDEL,
USMC (RETIRED)
&
JEROME R. STRAYVE, JR.

WHAT READERS ARE SAYING ABOUT
BROKEN PROMISES

… If President Lincoln were alive today, he would say, "Shame on you RCS! Thank you LtCol Blickwedel for revealing the traitors in our midst in order to restore and reestablish a promise, now broken, to be broken no more.

— Father Joseph G. Luisi, Jefferson Hospital Chaplain

Counselors are trained to keep ethical standards regarding the progress and duration of therapy. Unrealistic performance standards strain this ethical bond of trust between veterans and their counselors, and actually hinder the healing process. This book is a 'must read' to raise awareness and to inspire the reader to prevent further erosion of healing at the VET Centers and in many other arenas where misapplied corporate models treat workers and those they care for as objects.

— Clarisse DiCandia, Clinical Psychologist
VET Center Counselor

… The description of the failures in the mental health care of veterans and the self-preservation defenses thrown up by the supervisory professionals in charge, trigger my own painful memories of emotional traumas and isolation in trying to receive adequate mental health services when I left the Corps. As I read, the more frustrated I became and the more I identified with the veterans who had been underserved to meet "quotas." It is a raw wound that has not yet started to heal …

— David J. Millush, Marine Corps Veteran

The system designed to heal the horrific emotional wounds of battle is clearly broken. ... The resistance and the dysfunction at his VET Center to deliver quality care went against the very mission of the Veterans Administration. Ted's perseverance to address the inadequacies and then ultimately getting the attention of three powerful Congressmen, demonstrates the character of true heroes ... Keep reading, and keep following the progress of the VET Center Improvement Act ...

—Andrew Eanniello, LtCol, USMC, Retired

It has taken a great deal of courage on Ted's part and personal suffering to move through the system to come to the successful outcome of motivating official legislation for improvement in the huge Veterans Administration ... Thank you for the privilege of sharing your painful yet jubilant journey

—Dame Dr. Effie Chow, RN, PhD in Higher Education

... He has single-handedly taken on the largest healthcare institution in the country – the Veterans Health Administration. This is a fascinating read and engages the reader to join the fight. As one who has worked for a short time in the VET Center program and 27 years as Chief of Chaplain Service for the VA Boston Healthcare System, I can attest that what Blickwedel exposes is factual and all encompassing ...

—Father Philip G. Salois, Vietnam Combat Veteran
Vietnam Veterans of America National Chaplain

The system designed to heal the horrific emotional wounds of battle is clearly broken. Ted Blickwedel ... courageously and forcefully spoke up. He was met with vindictive retaliation. This book tells his story. ... showing how the system can resist even the most obvious solutions and chronicling the way one whistleblower's persistence unfolded as an inspiring and triumphant journey.

—David Feinstein, Ph.D.
Author, *The Ethics Handbook for Energy Healing Practitioners*

DEDICATION

Broken Promises is dedicated to all our veterans and active military for their sacrifice in service to this country to protect our freedom and way of life. It is also devoted to all former and current VA clinicians and VET Center counselors for their diligence, commitment, and compassion in the care they have given and continue to provide for our veterans and their families.

AUTHORS' NOTE

Many interviews were conducted while researching *Broken Promises*. These interviews provided much of the information used to write this book, humanizing what is, on its face, an inhuman and cold miscarriage of justice. The authors hope sharing excerpts from hundreds of hours of input provided by involved sources will prove meaningful to our readers in their appreciation of this arduous journey.

The reader should also be aware documentation is available at *www. VAbreakingpromises.com* in the *References* Tab which substantiates actions, events and experiences portrayed in *Broken Promises* for transparency. This includes emails, documents, and reports contained or quoted in the text, as well as evidence not directly cited.

CONTENTS

INTRODUCTION

Broken Promises was written to expose the harmful and unethical performance standards imposed by the Department of Veterans Affairs (VA) management on clinicians in the VET Center program, as well as disclose the damaging impact this has had on counselor welfare and mental health services for veterans. It further reveals the unjust, deceptive, and hostile retaliation tactics used by VA leadership to silence, marginalize, and stigmatize those who address these issues, including the extensive and devastating effect these reprisals have on them, their families, colleagues, and the clients they serve.

The ultimate purpose, however, is to inspire others to have hope and be compelled to fulfill their moral obligation for the common good by reporting government and corporate misconduct and abuse, promoting positive change and supporting those involved in these efforts, even when faced with what appears to be insurmountable odds at great sacrifice. This is portrayed by sharing one whistleblower's tenacious and agonizing journey in speaking truth to power, who eventually obtained the support of Congress through initiating legislation enhancing the preservation of quality care for veterans and ensuring that the well-being of dedicated staff who serve them is not compromised in America's largest integrated health care system.

The final objective of this book is to firmly encourage advocates and politicians to endorse strong Congressional legislation which truly provides full support and protection for whistleblowers, with severe consequences that are actually enforced for individuals and organizations who retaliate against them.

Overall, it is imperative to clarify that the intent of Broken Promises is not to vilify the VA or the VET Center program, but to ensure that the outstanding services offered by its very competent counselors to our veterans does not continue to be jeopardized by the VA leadership's improper emphasis on excessive quantitative clinical measures when it should be more focused on the quality of therapeutic interventions.

CHAPTER 1

Life and Death

His head spun as he reached for the doorjamb leading to the master bathroom. The room darkened and faded, then everything went black. His body slammed against the bathroom's solid oak door, crashing it into the bathroom wall. He crumpled to the floor. The resulting thud reverberated out of the bathroom and into the bedroom, echoing down the hall to the family room and kitchen.

"Honey," Julie yelled, "what was that noise?"

Several seconds passed as she continued to rinse the breakfast dishes and place them in the dishwasher.

"Ted?"

She placed the detergent pod in the dishwasher, slammed the door, and called again, her voice quivering. "Ted! Did you hear me?"

She hurried out of the kitchen toward the bedroom.

"Answer me, honey!"

Entering the master bedroom, the light from the bathroom illuminated Ted's body sprawled on his back on the tiled bathroom floor. Julie rushed across the room and dropped to her knees next to her husband's unconscious form. Her face ashen and her hands clammy,

1

she knelt caressing his face, her mind careening wildly through every possible scenario. *Was he dead? Dying? What do I do? He's much too big for me to carry or lift him. Think, Julie!*

Ted's eyes fluttered, then opened halfway.

"Ted, what's wrong? What do you want me to do? Call an ambulance?"

He stared up at her, his eyes unfocused.

She said decidedly in a cadenced voice, "I'm calling 911!"

He took several breaths and murmured, "No, just get me to the bed; I'll be okay."

Ignoring him, Julie sprang to her feet and ran to the kitchen, picked up her phone and dialed 911. After what seemed an eternity, she heard a voice come on the line. Julie interrupted the operator and stuttered, "Help me, please! My husband's collapsed. He might have had a heart attack or a stroke!" After providing their address she flew back to the bedroom.

Ted was inching toward the bed on all fours.

"Honey, stop, stay where you are, the paramedics are on their way."

Julie dropped to her knees, wrapped her arm around his shoulders and pleaded, "Please, honey, stop. You might fall again, and I can't pick you up. Please stop, lay back down!"

Ted lifted one hand in protest.

Julie pleaded, "Please, honey, if you fall …"

He grunted, "Julie, I know what I am doing."

She gave into his pleas, steadied her adrenalin-charged, 95-pound frame and helped him rise and stumble to the bed.

Julie rubbed her hands together. The room was cold. Staring down at the bed, she wished she had brought a sweater.

2

Both blinking lights on the monitors synchronized with the beep, beep, beep sounds bouncing off the beige-colored ICU walls.

Secured by safety rails, Ted lay unconscious on the hospital bed. A breathing tube snaked from his nose and various IVs were attached to his arms.

Julie stood beside her unconscious husband; her son Chris next to her holding her hand.

"Did you reach Michelle?" Julie asked Chris while reflexively straightening the sheets.

"Yeah, Sis is on her way."

A doctor drew back the privacy curtain and introduced himself. Addressing Julie, he said "Mrs. Blickwedel, I know you have many questions, and I am here to answer all of them. If I do not have the answer, I will return with one as soon as possible. If you do not mind, I will tell you what I do know, then feel free to ask me anything you like. Is that okay with you?"

Julie tilted her head, making strong eye contact with the doctor and said, "Yes, of course. Thank you."

The doctor smiled kindly and continued, "Your husband is lucky to be alive." He paused for a moment, then continued, "Your husband has suffered a Submassive Pulmonary Saddle Embolism."

"A what?" Julie asked, her eyes now pleading.

The doctor paused and swallowed. "It appears he has clotting in his pulmonary artery."

Julie blurted out, "What is Pulmonary, what does that mean? Will he be okay?"

"Pulmonary means the problem is in his lungs. This is an unusual situation. Normally, the outlook in situations like this is not promising, but your husband's case is unique. He is very strong, and that strength works in his favor. It is quite possible he will beat the odds. I am very hopeful."

Julie nodded slowly, her eyes appearing to glaze. Chris took his free hand and placed it over the one caressing his mother's hand.

"Submassive, that means serious, doesn't it?" Chris asked.

"It does," the doctor replied, glancing at the clipboard he'd brought with him when he'd entered the hospital room. He moved to the wall of monitors next to Ted saying, "The pulmonary artery carries deoxygenated blood from the right side of the heart to the lungs. His lungs are blocked."

Chris interrupted, "That means his heart isn't getting the blood it needs to send to the lungs so that he will get oxygen, right?"

"Yes," the doctor said, scanning the monitors. "Essentially, both lungs are partially blocked, and his heart is not functioning fully. We know one clot is lodged in his upper chest and only the right side of his heart is functioning. Our immediate concern is that we are not sure how many clots there are, or where they are. They might break loose and cause a heart attack."

Julie swallowed hard. "What can you do to stop that?"

Facing Julie, the doctor said in a mildly upbeat tone, "We have given him blood thinners, Mrs. Blickwedel. We will keep a close eye on him, you can count on that."

Ted's second day in the hospital found his doctors confronting the VA hospital's lack of sufficient resources. The doctors determined they did not have the personnel or equipment to adequately care for him should a clot reach his heart. A decision was made to transfer him to the 719-bed Rhode Island Hospital in Providence.

In an interview sometime later, Ted recalled the trip to the VA Hospital:

> I'm thinking, wow, this has really gotta be serious. And if
> something were to happen now, before I get to the hospital,
> I'm outta Schlitz. So yeah, it was … a very delicate moment.
> And I think they were actually worried—without really saying
> anything to me directly—about the transport and getting me
> there and something not getting dislodged in the transport.

Later, having been transferred to the Rhode Island Hospital, Ted
recalled:

> They get me situated in ICU and now I'm back on the heparin
> drip and feeling better. So, I'm feeling better in the sense that if
> something were to have happened and they had to rush me into
> surgery, at least I'm where I need to be for them to do something.

Ted recounted he had felt in good hands at the VA Hospital and then
expressed the same feelings about the Rhode Island Hospital:

> Again, at that point, I again felt in good hands, in fact, so
> much so I actually had my wife bring my cell phone and some
> documents that I had been working on to the hospital. I actually
> was continuing to work and make calls regarding all these
> advocacy efforts I was moving forward on, the concerns I was
> fighting for regarding the VA's excessive metrics and counselor
> burnout and the compromising of quality mental health care.

Ted remained at the Rhode Island Hospital for two days. Once
the doctors felt the danger of the clot dislodging had passed, he was
transferred back to the Veteran's Hospital. He spent two days there
and was sent home with a prescription for a blood thinner, Xarelto.

As part of the interview process, Ted was also asked, "So, what was going on in your head? You're recovering, you've come home. You're aware that you obviously had a life-or-death kind of situation?"

Ted responded:

If I may say, what's really interesting was, I was very scared when I got discharged from the hospital, I was scared. I was actually more scared upon my discharge than I was when I went in and was going through all that, 'cause, I remember feeling like, very insecure, you know, lack of confidence at being discharged where I thought it was too soon, even though they put me on Xarelto and had diluted that clot. I was just concerned like, wow. Yeah. You know, here I am, I'm being discharged. I'm getting this medication. I felt very uneasy, very unsure of myself, and to the point, I was afraid to be alone and everywhere I went in the house, I kept the phone with me in case I had to speed dial, you know, not type in 9-1-1. And if Julie had to leave, which I didn't, I didn't like her leaving me alone, but she had to go out and run errands. That first week or two, I felt really uneasy. So, whenever she left, we kept the door open and unlocked in case something happened and the EMT had to come back.

Ted believes he does not have a proclivity for blood clots and agrees with his doctors in their speculation that depression had led to a sedentary lifestyle, ushering in a decline in his health that brought on the embolism. This was due to the emotional trauma he suffered from retaliation-related stress.

He explains his depression in the following manner:

The two months leading up to that [the embolism] and enduring the VA VET Center management's forced isolation, distancing, marginalizing, gaslighting, and trying to silence me with all the retaliation tactics the VA was using against me—and the betrayal I felt it was worse and more traumatic than any combat experiences I had. They cut me down. I was so angry and depressed. The VA VET Center management had broken their promise to veterans, and in my fight to right their wrong, the severe impact from their toxic reprisals almost killed me.

CHAPTER 2

The Broken Promise

At the heart of this matter is the promise President Abraham Lincoln made to veterans following the Civil War: "To care for him who shall have borne the battle, and for his widow, and his orphan."

If *The Promise* had never been broken, clients and counselors would never have been confronted with the cruel and deadly consequences of VET Center management's self-serving, ill-advised, and professionally devastating policy change.

Had VET Center management responded to the actual concerns voiced by counselors, whistleblowing would not have been necessary. Congressional legislation would not be required to reinstate The Promise, protecting veterans and counselors from the VET Center management tasked with serving them.

(The following is taken from https://www.va.gov/about_va/mission.asp)

The VA Mission Statement

"To care for him who shall have borne the battle, and for his widow, and his orphan, by serving and honoring the men and women who are America's veterans."

Core Values

The VA's five core values underscore the obligations inherent in its mission: Integrity, Commitment, Advocacy, Respect, and Excellence. The core values define "who we are, our culture, and how we care for veterans and eligible beneficiaries. Our values are more than just words—they affect outcomes in our daily interactions with veterans and eligible beneficiaries and with each other. Taking the first letter of each word—Integrity, Commitment, Advocacy, Respect, Excellence—creates a powerful acronym, 'I CARE,' that reminds each VA employee of the importance of their role in this Department. These core values come together as five promises we make as individuals and as an organization to those we serve."

Integrity: Act with high moral principle. Adhere to the highest professional standards. Maintain the trust and confidence of all with whom I engage.

Commitment: Work diligently to serve veterans and other beneficiaries. Be driven by an earnest belief in VA's mission. Fulfill my individual responsibilities and organizational responsibilities.

Advocacy: Be truly veteran-centric by identifying, fully considering, and appropriately advancing the interests of veterans and other beneficiaries.

Respect: Treat all those I serve and with whom I work with dignity and respect. Show respect to earn it.

Excellence: Strive for the highest quality and continuous improvement. Be thoughtful and decisive in leadership, accountable for my actions, willing to admit mistakes, and rigorous in correcting them.

It is not the purpose of this book to defile the Department of Veterans Affairs. By definition, this agency exists to serve our veterans. It has and is a critical and valuable resource for veterans. The VA has been invaluable in serving veterans. One of the purposes of this book is to identify a great wrong perpetrated by management in the VET Center program, to rectify the wrong and to make good on The Promise made by Abraham Lincoln and Congress.

The Department of Veterans Affairs is made up of three administrations:

- **Veterans Health Administration** (VHA): responsible for providing health care in all its forms, as well as for biomedical research (under the Office of Research and Development), Community-Based Outpatient Clinics (CBOCs), Regional Medical Centers (VAMC), and Readjustment Counseling Services (RCS) VET Centers.
- **Veterans Benefits Administration** (VBA): responsible for initial veteran registration, eligibility determination, and the five key lines of business (benefits and entitlements):
  - Home Loan Guarantee

- Insurance
- Vocational Rehabilitation and Employment
- Education (GI Bill)
- Compensation & Pension
- **National Cemetery Administration:** responsible for providing burial and memorial benefits, as well as for maintenance of VA cemeteries.

The RCS VET Center program is a quasi-independent arm of the Veterans Administration. By design, it is administered separately from the VA. This accommodation was made to personalize and create community-based counseling centers. Each of these centers, embedded in communities, are configured to facilitate an intimate setting conducive to Veterans acquiring informal, yet professional counseling.

One of this book's interviewees could not have said it better when asked about being offered counseling by Ted Blickwedel at the VET Center:

Well, first of all, seeing I knew he was a Marine was a big plus for me because we take care of each other. Right. And it was, I could tell, as soon as I met him that his man was gonna help me. Okay. It was his demeanor, his tone, his stature.

From the very beginning, the VET Center upper-level management was almost entirely staffed by veterans. Each of the centers were managed by a director who also provided counseling. In large part, almost all the directors and counselors were Vietnam veterans.

As years passed, Vietnam veterans serving at all levels in the VET Center program aged out and/or retired. Their ranks were, in part, filled by counselors having served in combat in ensuing wars and conflicts.

The VET Center culture stayed largely intact for three decades. Then it changed. Today, fewer than half of those serving in the VET Centers are veterans.

Veterans suffer from a host of different mental and/or emotional struggles, such as PTSD, Traumatic Brain Injury (TBI) and depression, and are conflicted on many different levels. Suffice it to say, the personal and customized approach advocated by VET Center site directors and counselors when dealing with individual clients was the only effective course of action. Each individual VET Center location director was traditionally allowed to run their facility according to the needs of its veteran clients. Such was the case until March 1, 2016.

On March 1, 2016, a memorandum was distributed via email to lower management and counselors throughout the 300 plus VET Centers scattered across all 50 states.

This memorandum essentially mandated counselors increase the number of clients they saw by 50 percent. Practically applied, this required counselors to limit time spent with individual clients and *make it up* in group sessions.

Trust is paramount when counseling veterans. Acquiring that trust is often a painstaking, time-consuming, and incremental process. Though typically scheduled for 50–60 minutes, counseling sessions often run over that time. When establishing a rapport and garnering trust, time can be the enemy.

Individuals suffering from combat-related trauma are frequently emotionally fragile. The March 1, 2016, VET Center management policy change is essentially intransigent by design, making it unrealistic for counselors to cater to many veteran's needs.

When interviewing veterans, the common thread is the veteran's initial reluctance to first, admit their problems and second, to seek help. The initial makeup of the VET Center program had built in the flexibility to garner veterans' trust. It required counselors to assess the needs of their clients and take the time and make the effort to meet those needs. Granted, many counselors worked far more hours than the 40 they were paid for each week. The counselors were and remain the catalyst that keeps The Promise.

Over time, trust was established between the client and counselor. This hard-earned trust facilitated effective treatments. Many of these client/counselor relationships lasted for years.

One of Ted's clients, a Vietnam vet stated:

> I could never give my trust to any counselors that I dealt with in the past, but for some reason, and I think a lot of it could have been because of my counselor's military background— never talked about his military background but did talk that he was in the service for many years, very highly respected officer in the Marines. I just felt talking to him was much easier though. It took me months, months to talk to him about the things that would eat me up for many, many, many years. And over the course of many years, I continued going to my counselor monthly. And if I needed anything in between sessions, he was always so cordial to me and never once said to me, "Listen, just tell me everything." Never pushed me to do anything. In fact, he was always more of an instructor showing and telling me different ways that he believed would help me to get everything out. And more importantly, kept my head on straight. And he did that. It took years, but he did it. He let me do it my way and was always there for me. There for me at any time, day or night.

This relationship exemplifies the rapport veterans seeking mental health counseling have had with their counselors.

Then, without warning or notice, the new policy was put into effect. Clients were caught off guard. It was if the hard-won trust had ruptured, or certainly became compromised. A chasm opened up and swallowed the confidence in the counselors many veterans had embraced. Veterans felt as if they were teetering on the edge.

The policy changes shoved down counselors' throats placed them in untenable situations bewildering their clients. No longer could the counselors prioritize client mental health above the production numbers VET Center management demanded.

The veterans undergoing counseling were not initially made aware of the policy change. Suddenly counselors appeared less relaxed, more purposeful, and less engaged. The feeling of being short-changed became most apparent when 45 or 50 minutes had passed during counseling sessions. Counselors would either look at their watch or glance at the clock. The veteran soon learned no matter where they were in their counseling session, their time was up.

This newly mandated policy rattled a number of veterans. They assumed the counselors suddenly did not really care about their well-being. Some veterans felt betrayed, foolish, and insignificant, thus fueling an already turbulent emotional state.

A former VET Center client shared what she felt when she first noticed a change in her counselor:

> I had been seeing my counselor for several years. Then I noticed a difference in her. It wasn't gradual, it happened all at once, maybe the summer of 2016, I think. Maybe earlier. Something was going on, but I felt it's not my place to ask. And I always used to tell her, I feel as though my problems are a burden, burdening me, burdening you.

Interactions and statements from many interviewees painted the same picture of clients throughout the VET Center program experiencing the same shift in client/counselor interactions.

As a result, many clients terminated their relationship with the VET Centers. In several documented and in an untold number of undocumented instances, the consequences of abandoning their vital counseling sessions proved tragic.

One veteran said:

> It was as if the cold, unfeeling arm of the old VA projected prior to the VET Centers being founded, had wrapped its evil arm around them once again.

Another veteran shared that he felt his stomach turn the first time he recognized that his counselor was not listening as closely as he had in the past. For the first time, the counselor was taking notes and periodically looking at his watch.

> Think of it, a big rug had been pulled out from under me. I did not know it at the time, but I was internalizing that after all this time and sharing my most intimate secrets, my greatest fears, I was nothing but a number. I never went back for counseling. I am not sure if that was the right move, but I no longer trusted him. I liked him, sure. I did not know about the policy change. I just knew that something awful had happened. I ran away. My nightmares came back.

A longtime client, teary-eyed, recounted after asked if he regretted not going back for counseling because he felt like a number said:

> Yeah. In ways I do and otherwise I don't, but I know all that was going on there. And I'm not saying this because of my counselor, but I, when having gone for so many years and then you, all of a sudden feel the pressure they are under, and I'm not a psychiatrist, but I can tell you from the office

person right on down, things changed. They weren't like they used to be; it was always relaxed. It was never like a bell. And somebody said, "[W]ell, time's up." It was never like that. I … I … I don't know. Maybe I'm wrong. I … I think there was times when he and I talked for a couple hours and now, all of a sudden, things were all tanked. I … I … I'm a good judge of character, and I can tell my counselor had a lot to deal with, and I'm not a psychiatrist.

Consequences of the policy change were not limited to veterans. Some of the most devastating ramifications can be found in how counselors were negatively impacted professionally and personally.

CHAPTER 3

About Ted

Theodore Roosevelt and Theodore "Ted" Blickwedel have many things in common. They both possess courage and an unabashed commitment to their morals. Transparency and a passionate, hard-charging persona in the face of adversity frame both men's modus operandi.

Speaking truth to power, Theodore Roosevelt confronted major corporations, championed conservation of natural resources and advocated for consumer protection. All this vis-à-vis overwhelming opposition.

Ted Blickwedel spoke truth to power in his quest to keep the promise made by Congress to serve veterans. He went up against the management in the largest agency in the world, the Veterans Administration.

Roosevelt did not sit back and acquiesce to the powerful interests of his time. He disregarded naysayers and ultimately lost his bid for reelection while relentlessly pursuing his crusades to right wrongs.

Blickwedel also did not give in to the shunning, marginalizing, gaslighting, mobbing/bullying, and recriminations forced on him by

VET Center management. At the same time, he suffered professionally, and his mental and physical health were compromised, resulting in his retirement from the VET Center three years earlier than he had planned.

Even in defeat, the 26th President of the United States continued advocating for policies he felt were deeply important.

In retirement, Blickwedel continues to march forward, headfirst, continuing the fight for veterans and counselors. Down, but not out, his efforts led to members of the US Senate and House of Representatives sponsoring legislation to protect veterans and counselors within the VET Center program and forever hold accountable those who had so cold-heartedly broken The Promise.

Ted Blickwedel was born and raised in a blue-collar family in Pennsylvania. His commitment to his education and to his country laid the foundation for his moving steadfastly through life.

Ted's childhood was anything but idyllic and, in fact, emotional and physical childhood trauma helped prepare him for his life's challenges.

> It's as if in some weird sort of way, my life followed a path that was preparing me for all that I would encounter in fighting for veterans and bringing truth to power. Not only did I experience PTSD as a child, but also in combat. Life experiences made me stronger, preparing me to become more resilient and resolute. Through my own PTSD-related challenges, I was better prepared to understand the complexities and vagaries associated with what my clients and other counselors were experiencing.

Ted is a retired Lieutenant Colonel in the United States Marine Corps who is also a combat and disabled veteran. Prior to working as a VET Center counselor at the VA, he received a BA in Psychology (1977) and a Master's of Education in Rehabilitation Counseling (1978) from Penn State University.

From 1979 to 1983, Ted served on full-time active duty with the Marine Corps as a logistics officer before joining the Marine Corps Reserves. He performed intermittent extended periods of active duty in diverse assignments under the Active Duty Special Works Program from 1984 to 2006. During this period, Ted also served in the Persian Gulf War with the 10th Marine Regiment in 1991. Additionally, in 2003, he was mobilized out of the Individual Ready Reserves in support of Operation Enduring Freedom and again in 2005 in support of Operation Iraqi Freedom.

Following his retirement from the Marine Corps in 2006, he attended Rhode Island College for two years and obtained a Master's Degree in Clinical Social Work (MSW) in 2008.

Subsequently, Ted conducted individual and group therapy with combat veterans from January 2009 until February 2018 at the Warwick, Rhode Island VET Center for the Readjustment Counseling Service (RCS).

During his tenure in the Marine Corps, Ted met and married his wife, Julie Odal, and helped raise Michelle and Chris, her two young children from a previous marriage.

CHAPTER 4

A Little History

Understanding the background, history, and makeup of the Department of Veterans Affairs is integral to comprehending and internalizing the deeply personal issues permeating *Broken Promises*. The VA VET Center program management and counselor staff has traditionally been comprised of male and female veterans. This unique component is singularly responsible for the Centers having effectively met the needs of fellow veterans through keeping The Promise Abraham Lincoln espoused.

> *"To care for him who shall have borne the battle,*
> *and for his widow, and his orphan."*

VET Center counselors, serving their comrades, have walked the same walk. In many cases, veteran counselors and their clients have confronted similar issues. The bond, the camaraderie and singularly unconditional and uncompromising purpose-driven connection has fostered extraordinarily successful treatments throughout the VET Center program. These successes did not come without a price. Both parties, client and counselor, had to trust and believe in one another. Trust is hard won, but once achieved, this foundation built on trust has supported tremendous gains in mental health counseling.

Faith in, and hope for, one's fellow veteran has propelled this cadre of VET Center counselors to work long, grueling hours in their quest to serve their clients. Their work hours were not limited to the normal 9–5 workday, but often included early mornings, late evenings and weekends.

VET Center counselors are predominately social workers and psychologists with a passion for their profession that is, in most instances, more a lifestyle than a job.

During his nine-year tenure as a counselor, Ted Blickwedel was the epitome of this type of counselor. One of his former clients could not have said it better.

> Colonel Blickwedel saved my life. I'm not kidding. If it were not for him, I would not be here today. I love that man like a brother. I do not trust people. I don't really like people that much. He got me from the beginning. I didn't trust him or anyone. He put up with my crap for a long time, months. Why he didn't throw me out of his office, I have no idea. I just couldn't believe there was someone who could or would help me. I must have known deep down, but...anyway, one day I decided to open up. I did, and to make a long story short, I did not off myself because I had finally found someone I could trust. Someone who could help me. He worked with me for years until those bastards fucked him over. But he did a good job. Because here I am, four years later, doing okay.

Congress passed legislation 40 years ago to address the needs Vietnam veterans had expressed for a more personalized and dynamic way to obtain counseling. At that time, the need was not being met within the Veterans Administration, which became the Department of Veterans Affairs in 1989 when President Reagan elevated it to cabinet level and appointed the first VA secretary.

Readers are certainly aware of the Byzantine-like fabric that has and remains embodied in the VA. The organization is the largest health care agency in the world. Inherent in this are the challenges confronting the agency in addressing the very personal needs of its clientele. Vietnam veterans returned from what was truly one of the most barbaric wartime scenarios known to man in modern warfare.

The conflict began in 1954 and raged through 1975. The fighting stemmed from the Indochina War originating in 1946 and culminated in the French departing the region in 1954. This conflict involved the French opposing independence and the Ho Chi Minh-led guerrilla warfare ending in the nationalist Vietnamese victory at Dien Bien Phu on May 7, 1954. Their victory resulted in the division of Vietnam into two countries along the 17th latitudinal parallel, the communist-led North Vietnam and the American-supported South Vietnam.

The United States became overtly involved in its military support of South Vietnam in the mid-1960s. A ceasefire was signed in January of 1973 and at that time, the US troops began to slowly withdraw. However, fighting between the two countries continued throughout

1975 when the communist-led North Vietnam ultimately defeated the democratic South Vietnam.

The American anti-war movement resulted in the military personnel returning home from Vietnam being villainized, ostracized, and effectively shunned by the country that had drafted a vast majority of them and sent them off to war. At no time in American history, and perhaps in all of history, had returning combatants been so ignominiously received by their countrymen.

War, by its nature, deeply scars those who survive battle. The long-term ramifications of physical and emotional injuries incurred are beyond comprehension. Men and women returning home from a hostile environment to encounter yet another virulent environment served to only exacerbate the emotional traumas ignited by war.

The RCS VET Center program falls under the Veterans Health Administration. As mentioned previously, the Veterans Health Administration (VHA) was ill-equipped to serve its veterans in caring for their emotional trauma, let alone physical injuries including, but not limited to, lost limbs, brain damage, and loss of sight and hearing.

VET Center History

Taken from *www.VETcenter.va.gov/About_US.asp*

> VET Centers' Readjustment Counseling Services were established by Congress in 1979 out of the recognition that a significant number of Vietnam era Veterans were

still experiencing readjustment problems. VET Centers are community-based and part of the U.S. Department of Veterans Affairs. In April 1991, in response to the Persian Gulf War, Congress extended eligibility to veterans who served during other periods of armed hostilities after the Vietnam era. Those other conflicts are identified as Lebanon, Grenada, Panama, the Persian Gulf, Somalia, and Kosovo/Bosnia.

In October 1996, Congress extended the eligibility to include WWII and Korean combat veterans. The goal of the VET Centers is to provide a broad range of counseling, outreach, and referral services to eligible veterans to help them make a satisfying post-war readjustment to civilian life. On April 1, 2003, the Secretary of Veterans Affairs extended eligibility for VET Center services to Veterans of Operation Enduring Freedom (OEF) and on June 25, 2003, Vet Center eligibility was extended to Veterans of Operation Iraqi Freedom (OIF) and subsequent operations within the Global War on Terrorism (GWOT).

The family members of all veterans listed above are eligible for VET Center services as well. On August 5, 2003, then VA Secretary Anthony J. Principi authorized VET Centers to furnish bereavement counseling services to surviving parents, spouses, children and siblings of service members who die of any cause while on active duty, including federally-activated Reserve and National Guard personnel.

Readjustment Counseling is a wide range of psycho/social services offered to eligible veterans, service members and their families in the effort to make a successful transition from military to civilian life. They include:

- Individual and group counseling for veterans, service members, and their families;
- Family counseling for military-related issues;
- Bereavement counseling for families who experience an active-duty death;
- Military sexual trauma counseling and referral;
- Outreach and education including PDHRA , community events, etc.;
- Substance abuse assessment and referral;
- Employment assessment and referral;
- VBA benefits explanation and referral;
- Screening and referral for medical issues including TBI, depression, etc.

The VA's Readjustment Counseling is provided at over 300 community-based VET Centers located in easily-accessible neighborhoods near veterans, service members, and their families, yet separate from VA organizational sites to ensure confidential counseling and to reduce barriers to care. All VET Center services are prepaid through military service.

CHAPTER 5

They Knew Better

In 2015, about a year prior to the announcement and implementation of the new productivity standards policy change, the Clinical Capacity Report was submitted to VET Center management.

The Clinical Capacity Report was compiled in February 2015 by an RCS VET Center Working Group made up of counselors and VET Center directors from each of the 5 RCS districts. The study identified shortfalls in the VET Center program to include excessive clinical productivity standards that they recognized would cause counselor burnout and adversely impact quality of care for veterans. During the study and analysis, and unbeknownst to the members of the working group, VET Center upper management was in the midst of planning and implementing a far-ranging policy procedure that would adversely affect the lives of veteran clients and counselors alike.

The formation of this working group confirmed productivity issues had been identified by a broad spectrum of counselors throughout the VET Center program. *This voluntary group of counselors and directors working in the field tasked themselves with studying the problem and developing a methodology with which to address and make recommendations on how to rectify a deteriorating work environment.*

The following excerpt from the report's executive summary will shed some light on why none of the recommendations by this intrepid group of counselors were adopted by management.

Our findings revealed many systemic failures across the program and at all levels from Central Office, Regional Offices and VET Centers. Each of these misfortunes has tremendous impact on clinical capacity.

The report, though never acknowledged, or implemented, foretold the inevitable.

In August 2019, a year and a half after Ted's retirement, as a consequence of VET Center managements' recriminations, one of the working group participants informed Ted and NBC News that none of the Clinical Capacity Report's suggestions had been incorporated into VA/RCS policy or guidelines.

And again, several VET Center counselors whom Ted spoke with shortly thereafter told him that the problems with productivity metrics had become even worse, as clinicians had been given additional administrative duties while being expected to achieve the March 1, 2016, increased performance standards mandate. The hammer fell via the following memorandum sent out to the VA VET Center field staff:

Department of Veterans Affairs

Date: March 1, 2016
From Acting Chief Officer, Readjustment Counseling Service
(10RCS)
Subject: VET Center Service Delivery Minimum Expectations
Assessment

To: Readjustment Counseling Service (RCS) District Director and Regional Managers

Effective immediately the following information will be distributed to all VET Centers.

PURPOSE: To provide RCS District and Regional leadership and VET Center Team Leaders with information regarding minimum service delivery expectations by staff providers.

SCOPE: This guidance is applicable to RCS staff members with responsibility for service delivery, supervision and/or quality oversight.

BACKGROUND PERSPECTIVES: This guidance emphasizes the responsibility of all RCS leadership to assess the provision and quality of readjustment counseling services on a consistent basis. These oversight activities are entirely grounded in support of the VET Center readjustment counseling mission for serving eligible veterans, service members, and their families.

The conceptual focus of readjustment counseling is the nexus between veterans' and service members' combat experience and their current life adjustment. Readjustment counseling addresses the psychological residue of unresolved traumatic combat experiences that impact post-war adjustments, including issues related to family, employment and career. The readjustment counseling service mission consists of three interrelated service functions: outreach, direct readjustment counseling, and referral and care coordination. Direct readjustment counseling is provided in three modalities: individual, group, and family.

VET Center oversight evaluation requires a combination quantitative measures and qualitative evaluations regarding the direct service mission. Quantitative measures include direct service visits provided to veterans, service members, and their families, SSN-verified outreach contacts, and the accurate accounting for time within the RCS Network. Quality of care evaluations include annual site visits, assessment of the VET Center Team Leader's supervision; the efficacy of the VET Center's non-institutional, personally engaging atmosphere promoting collegial relationships between staff and the local veteran community; and the strength of VET Center community relations and partnerships, VA and non-VA.

VET CENTER DIRECT SERVICE EXPECTATIONS: Specific expectations for VET Center staff are as follows:

Team Leaders: Fifteen (15) hours per week (37.5% RCSNet) in direct provision of readjustment counseling with an expectation of 1.5 visits per hour (average 40-hour week = 15 hours direct service, 22.5 visits).

Counselors: Twenty (20) hours per week (50% RCSNet) in direct provision of readjustment counseling with an expectation of 1.5 visits per hour (average 40-hour week = 20 hours direct service, 30 visits).

Note: Each hour of face-to-face service results in 1.5 documented readjustment counseling visits when accounting for group readjustment counseling work (multiple clients during one time period).

Outreach Workers: 60% of actual hours available (PAID) are spent in primarily Outreach activities and secondarily in Direct Services (RCSNet).

THE MANAGEMENT OF UNUSED SERVICE AVAILABILITY:

For the purpose of assessment, VET Center unused availability is defined as the number of available visits (derived from available counseling hours) below the minimum workload expectations and outcomes for each counseling staff member on the team, i.e., counseling staff were available, but no visits were documented.

Available counseling hours for each staff providing service are derived directly from the VA PAID system. Available hours are the total hours minus all non-duty hours annual leave, sick leave, etc. Only available hours are utilized.

All staff below 85% of their individualized expectation are required to develop an improvement plan approved by their supervisor. In each case, the staff member will receive documented, supportive and ongoing performance improvement supervision.

It is the responsibility of RCS leadership at all levels to develop strategic plans, share best practices, and encourage team innovation sufficient to bring every RCS staff service provider up to the minimum expectation:

- Ensure appropriate staff composition,

- Ensure effective level of outreach,

- Ensure appropriate case assignment regarding clinical complexity,

- Ensure effective utilization of group readjustment counseling, and

- As indicated, ensure appropriate utilization of ancillary staff (interns, temp/term over-hires, etc.

VET Centers with significant levels of unused service availability (over 2,000 unused visits available) require a strategic remediation plan taking into consideration the provisions of paragraph 6.d. above.

CONCLUDING COMMENT: In conclusion, all RCS leadership and service providing staff are responsible for meeting minimum expectations. These expectations were developed with full attention to all aspects of the Vet Center direct service mission.

Charles M. Flora, LCSW-C

Facing push back from all corners of the country over the lack of clarity in the policy change, upper management was directly confronted by disenfranchised counselors when district level directors conducted clinical site visits at VET Centers within their respective regions.

"Deal with it," they were told.

Other reactions were masked with feigned concern and more *heels dug in* emails not so effectively clarifying their self-proclaimed *mandate*.

Here is one more attempt at explaining how site directors were to *deal with* implementing their own requirement to manage their office and counsel veterans:

Team Leader Minimum

15 direct service hours per week

22.5 visits per week

1170 visits per year

Action Plan Trigger (yellow light) < 19 visits per week (below 85 percent of target)

Counselor Minimum

20 direct service hours per week

30 visits per week

1560 visits per year

Action Plan Trigger (yellow light) < 25.5 visits per week (below 85 percent of target)

Outreach

60 percent of hours available in outreach

24 hours outreach per week

Action Plan triggers (yellow light) < 20 hours per week (below 85 percent of target)

Translating the policy from bureaucratic-speak to plain English essentially means this: 20 hours out of a 40-hour work week is expected to be direct contact with clients involving 30 visits. The minimum number of visits required is 85% of this target which is 25.5 visits per week (30 X .85). If you don't meet this bottom-line quota, you are subject to reprimand which could lead to disciplinary action through a labor relations process.

Further implications: 25.5 to 30 client visits are to occur within 20 hours. The industry standard is that counselors spend 50–60 minutes with clients. This means that it would take 25.5 hours per week to achieve the minimum required visits. However, often 75–90-minute sessions are necessary to implement evidenced-based trauma treatment interventions which are needed by many veterans. This translates to 30 or more hours of direct client contact being required to accomplish this. That only leaves about 10 hours per week to complete progress notes, treatment plans, assessments, case consults, and other administrative duties. Many counselors work through their lunch period and more than 40 hours per week to complete all their tasks, even though they have been informed that they are not permitted to work overtime.

Interviews with various counselors found they were dumbfounded. On the face of it, they were encouraged to *pad the numbers* vis-à-vis group sessions. Some did indeed take that route so they would not lose their jobs, even though many veterans do not want to participate in groups. Others chose to right the wrong. Ted Blickwedel led that charge.

Here is the assessment of a former counselor, also recently forced into retirement, who shared the following upon learning of the policy change:

> By late 2016, the VA measurables changed and this stressed the therapeutic relationships between clinicians and patient/ veterans and their families. This increased the already strained relationships with line staff and the administration, as it began to cross lines and boundaries of ethical guidelines set

by NASW (National Association of Social Workers). *However, the VA executed changes, and this was without warning to the populations we served, causing clinicians to sacrifice personal and discipline-focused ethics for fear of reprisal.*

When asked about his initial thoughts personally and professionally, the counselor answered:

Disbelief that this was legal, wise, and in line with VA Core Values: Integrity, Commitment, Advocacy, Respect and Excellence. Much like today when the VET Center program removed 'Keeping the Promise' from its logo. Incredible! They knew they were breaking The Promise! It was intentional, planned! It was lame of the administration.

"What was your impression on the way in which your concerns or the concerns of others were handled by therapists and management?"

Therapists/clinicians were not valued as professionals unless you were proved a sycophant and willing to sacrifice self-values and good sound ethics that govern our profession. Most others were operating on sheer fear; fear for employment/income/career. However, many often complained and across the board figured out ways to permeate and go through the motions as well as fudge their own numbers to keep the administration at a distance. This decreased the quality of care we were able and capable of providing. The policy change resulted in an immediate interruption to the veteran patient and their family's care. The change was felt immediately, resulting in burnout. Conformity and stress were soon to follow.

A current VET Center director, fearful of reprisals, requested anonymity but told us:

> Everyone at the VET Center was concerned about the implementation of these standards. Saying to himself, How on earth are we going to do this? The major concern is by focusing on numbers, the VA was losing sight of the main priority—providing meaningful mental health services to veterans. These artificially induced standards will negatively affect the quality of mental health services that would be provided to Vets; that counselors are not going to be able to properly serve clients. While everyone was frustrated about these standards and let regional leadership know about their dissatisfaction, VA leadership really didn't do anything about the problems. I was told, 'It's a policy decision,' and essentially the counselors were just going to have to work with it. It just seemed that emphasis was on doing things faster-faster. Ironically, management would claim 'it's not about the numbers,' but it really is about the numbers now.

The director decided to retire early, in 2020.

In the summer of 2016, the National RCS VET Center Director Conference was held in Washington, DC. In a staff meeting held at the Warwick, RI VET Center, not long after that conference, Director Rochelle Fortin mentioned that numerous VET Center directors had expressed being depressed and experiencing some suicidal ideation.

This statement was made in the summer of 2016, several months after the policy change went into effect.

The VET Center program management team was quick to establish performance evaluations for the new policy. Up until the policy change had been implemented, performance evaluations were essentially the subjective domain of individual directors throughout the 300 plus VET Center locations. In the beginning, in the spirit of the creation of the VET Centers, individual center directors were encouraged to run their programs in accordance with their clients' needs. Importantly, at its inception, directors functioned not only as team leaders, but simultaneously had their own counselor caseloads.

Instructions from superior officers came with detailed metrics dictating the methodology for evaluating counselors' effectiveness in adhering to the new policy. In effect, what had once been a subjective and personalized employee evaluation, now became much more objective and a disconnected measurement designed to *achieve the numbers* requirement, as opposed to fulfilling The Promise and meeting the needs of veterans and their families.

Over the course of writing *Broken Promises*, interviews were conducted with former clients of the Warwick, RI VET Center and in several other cities. Finding veterans who were willing to sit down with the interviewer was not an easy task. Privacy and fragile emotional temperament proved to be the biggest impediment.

It is fair to say that these former clients have and will always have *open wounds*; wounds that are not limited to emotional, psychological, and in many instances physical disabilities. A vast majority of these wounds stem directly from military service. It is only fair to point out that many veterans were plagued with life events prior to joining the military, further compounding mental and emotional trauma suffered while in military service.

The following are comments taken from interviews conducted with former clients:

> Counselors quickly challenged the changes in policy. Their concerns were countered with management stating the policy had been in effect since the inception of the Vet Center. This begs the question, "Why had management not addressed the disparity long before, and had by implied consent, allowed the practice of meeting the needs of the veterans/clients at the discretion of directors and counselors for 37 years?"

Keeping The Promise required counselors to meet the needs of veterans.

The system that has been in place for 37 years is working. Why change it?

The VET Centers were established to implement much-needed personalized counseling. Each client has unique needs. Many of these needs are not readily discernible. Many, saddled with their individual challenges, were not equipped to work within the confines of 50–60-minute sessions. It quite frequently takes more than an hour to employ efficacious therapy strategies or conduct crisis interventions that are warranted.

Clinicians found that 60–90-minute sessions were often necessary to properly use conventional evidenced-based interventions to treat PTSD or other related traumas.

This dilemma was not uncommon. What was common were counselors recognizing what had to be done and then adjusting their schedules to accommodate the needs of their clients. To their credit, many counselors worked overtime without compensation to facilitate client's needs and fulfill ancillary duties.

The unique composition of veteran counselors and directors fostered a compassionate approach to serving their fellow veterans. This compassion underlying the culture fostered an unconditional and heartfelt bond.

Undoubtedly, the way counselors fought to serve their clients was unlike any other counseling services offered in private and other public health care services, health care services dominated by insurance companies dictating guidelines for their counselors.

Why on earth would a government agency, not saddled with the burden of showing a profit, adopt procedures anathema to their vision, purpose, and promise?

As the managers and counselors who had made up the first decades of the VET Center's staff retired, fewer and fewer were replaced with veterans. Institutional knowledge evaporated and the number of counselors having served in the military, many in combat, plummeted.

The VET Centers' new generation managers decided to implement the visit count standard, even though this decision flew in the face of the mission the VET Centers established in 1979.

The new policy changes effectively broke The Promise.

In a conversation with a retired VET Center director/counselor, she was asked about the effect on the quality care when implementing the clinical productivity mandates. She said:

The impact could very possibly and most probably compromise quality care. It depends on a lot of variables. It depends on the patient population at the moment. It depends on how you utilize individuals for group psychotherapy.

> It's just not a clear kind of thing. You know, if you see a patient once a week and you're asked not to see that patient once a week, because there isn't time, that's a compromise. I think that's a significant compromise. But if you know you've been seeing a patient for a long time and you know you've progressed along and now you can justify seeing him monthly, that has validity. It is vital you be able to adjust your caseload based on the needs of the clients. Under this policy change, it is a heavy burden.

Several current and former counselors said that prior to the new policy, some counselors were handling in excess of 100 clients per month. The National Association of Social Workers recommends counselor caseloads should normally not exceed 40 to 50 clients on a regular basis. It was not uncommon for RCS/VET Center counselors to have 70 to 80 clients.

Counselor burnout quickly escalated soon after implementation of the new policy. This resulted in counselors retiring early, seeking other employment, going into private practice or going out on disability. Rapidly, the percentage of counselors having served in the military diminished, further compromising veteran mental health care. The exodus of counselors in many centers was such that, in some instances, caseloads rose to over 80 to 100 clients. One former VET Center counselor reported his caseload increased to about 150 veterans. Hitherto, unanticipated early retirement of seasoned counselors was a big blow to the VET Center program.

Another conversation with a counselor brought forth the following:

> The clients are looking for someone to listen to them. But unfortunately, under this new arrangement, their time is up. Imagine yourself in their position: I'm looking for someone to

listen to me, but unfortunately time is up. That's what breaks a heart. That'll break a heart. Cause that's what it is all about, heart, compassion. And then there are the counselors and what they are dealing with. The counselor's heart is in what he is doing. And he was being prevented from letting his heart do its work. Wow. And, the counselor, well he may go a little crazy, frustrated, the care he has promised to provide is a sham. Counselors cannot help but take it personally. They are vets too, you know, serving their brothers and sisters.

Initially, Ted and his colleagues expressed their concerns to Warwick VET Center Director, Rochelle Fortin, about the quality of mental health services being compromised due to the excessive productivity performance expectations being placed on counselors. Ted and other clinicians assumed, per established protocol, that Ms. Fortin was forwarding their concerns to her supervisor at the District Office. However, it is not known if this ever occurred.

CHAPTER 6

Ted's Push Back

P ush back was a natural response for Ted Blickwedel when he was made aware of the compromising mental health care policy changes. These changes were and are contrary to The Promise made by the VA and subsequently broken by RCS VET Center management.

The blame does not initially fall on the Secretary of Veterans Affairs and his management team. But when made aware of the problem within the VET Center program, the VA went to the mat and appeared not to have made a discernible effort to mitigate the problem. Instead, they exacerbated it by stonewalling in the face of a GAO report validating Blickwedel's claims.

Ted was initially made aware of the policy change along with over a thousand counselors throughout the United States when all received the March 1, 2016, memorandum.

Like many other counselors, his first reaction was disbelief. His chief concern was adherence to these standards would interfere and compromise veteran's mental health care.

It is remarkable how a considerable number of counselors through-out the system came to the conclusion that the policy change was

43

imental to clients and counselors. Even more intriguing was at the same time the RCS VET Center senior management appeared to have little comprehension and no known empathy for the concerns being raised by frontline counselors and staff.

The overwhelming concerns that counselors were experiencing challenges complying with the new policy, both professionally and personally, came to light in the summer of 2016 at the National RCS Director Conference in Washington, DC.

Following the conference, Ms. Fortin, the Warwick RI Vet Center director and Ted Blickwedel's boss, shared with her staff that numerous VET Center directors expressed being depressed; some having suicidal ideation. Significantly, she said there were stories shared of clinical staff actually having committed suicide.

In an organization dedicated to treating mental health, why did the alleged suicides of clinical staff not raise alarm bells? Why did management not take steps to immediately respond to these obvious alarms?

In August of 2016, Ted began to feel depressed over not being able to provide the quality of care for his veterans due to the excessive pressure placed on counselors to produce the numbers mandated in the new policy. Ted shared in an interview that he knew he was not meeting the numbers.

> I had to meet the needs of my clients as I saw them. It is my spiritual, professional and ethical responsibility. I do not know any other way to do it. I would rather fail the system than fail my comrades, my clients.

In September of 2016, Rochelle Fortin directed Ted to complete a Performance Improvement Plan (PIP) as he had not met the clinical visit count expectations.

The PIP was then forwarded on to the RCS District 1 office. Essentially, Ted had been put on report for the first time in his career. Ted's depression was further triggered, and he soon found himself seeing a psychologist.

In 2016, the months of September, October, and November were an emotional roller-coaster ride for Ted. Previous issues from his childhood, then combat experiences, and finally the VET Center policy change denying him his ethical responsibility to provide adequate care, exploded onto the surface.

Simply put, the pressure and anxiety triggered issues he believed were long dormant.

The following is an excerpt from a mental health evaluation on Ted Blickwedel:

Date/Time: 14 Oct 2016@ 1149 Note Title: MH SAFE TY PLAN Location: PROVIDENCE RI VAMC Signed By: GATHRIGHT,EMILY CLAIRE Co-signed By: GATHRIGHT,EMILY CLAIRE Date/Time Signed: 14 Oct 2016@ 1212 -------------- LOCAL TITLE: MH SAFETY PLAN STANDARD TITLE: MENTAL HEALTH NOTE DATE

OF NOTE: OCT 14, 2016@1:149 ENTRY DATE: OCT 14, 2016@1:149:27AUTHOR: GATHRIGHT,EMILY CLA EXP COSIGNER: O'LEARY-TEVYAW,TRACY URGENCY: STATUS: COMPLETED SUICIDE SAFETY PLAN

STEP 1: RECOGNIZING WARNING SIGNS These signs indicate that I may be starting to get suicidal: 1. experiencing work-related stress 2. reminders of military/changes to military culture STEP 2: USING INTERNAL COPING STRATEGIES These activities may help me distract myself from thoughts about suicide: 1. mindfulness meditation exercise 2. going to the backyard STEP 3: SOCIAL CONTACTS WHO MAY DISTRACT

FROM THE CRISIS These social activities and people may help me distract myself from thinking about suicide:

1. wife 2. friend, Marge STEP 4: FAMILY OR FRIENDS WHO MAY OFFER HELP These are people that I would be willing to talk to about my thoughts of suicide in order to help me stay safe: NAME PHONE NUMBER 1. Marge keeps # in phone STEP 5: PROFESSIONALS AND AGENCIES TO CONTACT FOR HELP 1. Veteran will add new therapist to contact list upon initiation of treatment 2. Veteran provided with contact information for Emily Gathright, Psychology Resident, PCBH (Veteran in-formed of hours available) 24-hour emergency treatment: Call 911 Go to local Emergency Room 24-hour emergency VA Hotline: 1(800)273-TALK (8255) STEP 6: MAKING THE ENVIRONMENT SAFE These are steps I will take to limit access to means to kill myself: Veteran denied need to make changes to environment. Veteran feels that his environment is safe. There has been a discussion of the planning process with the veteran (and family involvement in process, if any). Veteran has been given a copy of this safety plan. PLAN REVIEW Suicide High Risk Treatment Plan will be reviewed: Plan to be reviewed at the next clinical visit and modified accordingly. Provider to notify Suicide Prevention Coordinator of any: status change, session, emergency, no show, PRN, of any Veteran on the facility High Risk for Suicide list. Veteran will be reevaluated for High Risk for Suicide list a mini-mum of every 90 days. /es/ EMILY CLAIRE GATHRIGHT Psychology Resident Signed: 10/14/2016 12:12 /es/ TRACY O'LEARY-TEVYAW, PH.D. CLINICAL PSYCHOLOGIST Cosigned: 10/14/2016 12:14 ==================================== == ====================== Date/Time· 14 Oct 2016@ 0936 Note Title: PRIMARY CARE BEHAVIORAL HEALTH/CONSULT Location: PROVIDENCE RI VAMC Signed By: GATHRIGHT,EMILY CLAIRE Co-signed By: GATHRIGHT,EMILY CLAIRE Date/Time Signed: 14 Oct 2016@ 1205 ---------------------------- LOCAL TITLE: PRIMARY CARE BEHAVIORAL HEALTH/CONSULT STANDARD TITLE: MENTAL HEALTH CONSULT DATE OF NOTE: OCT 14, 2016@09:36 ENTRY DATE: OCT 14, 2016@0:937:10 AUTHOR: GATHRIGHT,EMILY CLA EXP COSIGNER: O'LEARY-TEVYAW,TRACY URGENCY: STATUS: COMPLETED *** PRIMARY CARE BEHAVIORAL HEALTH/CONSULT Has ADDENDA *** PRIMARY CARE BEHAVIORAL HEALTH

ASSESSMENT BLICKWEDEL,THEODORE WILLIAM is a 61-year old NOT HISPANIC OR LATINO WHITE MALE veteran who presents for safety/risk assessment. Veteran was seen for 45 minutes. Veteran was referred by Dr. Plotkin for further evaluation and treatment recommendations for SI/depression. ASSESSMENT: Veteran reported increasing depression and frequent SI. Veteran rated mood as the "worst" in his life. Veteran expressed that over the past several months, he has felt increasingly hopeless as a result observing changes in the treatment of the military as well as work-related stress. Veteran reported plan to end his life by "going away for a few days" and dehydrating/starving himself. Veteran denied imminent risk. He cited a desire to get finances in order for his wife as a protective factor. Veteran stated that it will take him 18 to 24 months to do so. Veteran's wife is aware that he is experiencing depressive symp-toms, but is not aware of the extent or Veteran's SI. Veteran stated that he is currently attempting to be "proactive" to prevent further increase in SI intent. Veteran reported depressed mood, increased irritability, and difficulty sleeping. Veteran stated that he has "no purpose." Veteran engages in mindfulness meditation to cope with SI and feels that he can "experience" SI without acting on behavior. He described his "strong will" as a personal strength. Veteran shared that mindfulness has assisted Veteran in noticing thoughts without acting on them and stated that he has no intention of acting on current SI given current plans to resume psychotherapy and undergo evaluation to begin a psychotropic medication. Veteran reported previously suicidal plan/intent in the 1900s. Veteran intended to slit his wrists with a razorblade. Veteran was preparing to do so when he decided to call his friend, who "talked [him] out of it." Veteran's friend assisted him in reported primary social support to be his wife of 33 years. He has two step-children. Veteran currently lives at home with his wife. Veteran is employed as a social worker at the Vet center. Veteran does not believe his current symptoms are interfering with his functioning at work. He has been engaged in outpatient psychother-apy (primarily focused on therapies that target "energy" and mind-fulness). His former therapist moved and he is not followed current-ly. He has an appointment scheduled with a new therapist at the end of this month. Veteran not interested in pursuing psychotherapy services through VA. Veteran denied current substance use. Veteran reported history of heavy drinking. Veteran has not consumed alcohol is 5 years. Veteran is not on a psychotropic medication currently and would like to undergo an evaluation to begin an antidepressant. Veteran declined referral to Urgent Care today due to concerns related to involvement with individuals he may know. Veteran has no current or imminent plan or intent to harm self or end life and denied any recent attempts. Method of teaching was discussion. No barriers to learning were evident, and veteran appeared open and receptive to and understood material presented. SCREENING ASSESSMENT OF DANGER TO SELF/OTHERS: 1. Have you ever tried to seriously harm yourself in the past? Denied. 2. During the past month have you had any thoughts about harming yourself? Yes- see above. 3. During the past month have you harmed yourself or attempted suicide? Denied. 4. During the past month have you had any thoughts about harming someone else? Denied. Risk Factors: [X] yes [ ] no Hopelessness [x] yes [ ] no Access to means to carry out a plan [X] yes [ ] no Access to firearms [ ] yes [x] no Engaging in preparatory behaviors [ ] yes [X] no Acute/recent/impending loss: reported recent death of cousin [ ] yes [x no Worsening medical condition [ ] yes [X] no History of impul-sivity [ ] yes [x] no Substance Abuse [ ] yes [x] no Psychosis [ ] yes [x] no Chronic pain (pain score 6+) [ ] yes [X] no Anxiety/agitation [ ] yes [x] no Recent discharge from inpatient unit [ ] yes [x] no Family history of suicide Protective Factors: [X] yes [J no Social Supports: wife,friend (Marge) [ ] yes [X] no Therapeu-tic Alliance [X J yes [ ] no Dependent Children/Family/Pet Responsibility [X] yes [ ] no Future oriented Plans and Commitments [X] yes [ ] no Spirituality [X] yes [ ] no Good Problem Solving Skills Ability to maintain Safety independently without external supports [x] yes [ ] no Assessment of Suicide Risk: [ ] Low [X] Moderate [ ] High Assessment of Violence Risk: [X] Low [ ] Moderate [ ] High PERTINENT MEDICAL HISTORY: Active Problem History of adenomatous polyp of col 11/25/2014 OUELLETTE,JENNIFER R Hemangioma Skin 228.01 01/12/2014 BURNSIDE,NANCY J Inflamed Seborrheic Keratosis 702.1 01/12/2014 BURNSIDE,NANCY J Screen For Malignant Skin Neoplasm 01/12/2014 BURNSIDE,NANCY J Benign Neo Skin Trunk 216.5 01/12/2014 BURNSIDE,NANCY J Xerosis 706.8 01/12/2014 BURNSIDE,NANCY J Dermatitis or Eczema* (ICD-9-CM 69 06/25/2010 BURNSIDE,NANCY J Intertrigo 695.89 06/25/2010 BURNSIDE,NANCY

Ted's mental and emotional state declined to the point where he took more and more time off from work. His preoccupation with a lack of self-worth and bouts of suicidal ideation resulted in self-isolating. His doctor continued to increase the dosages of his antidepressant medication.

An online supervisory appointment scheduled between Ms. Fortin and Ted was canceled by Ms. Fortin and never rescheduled. Ted began to feel he did not belong at the VET Center. A meeting on the 19th of December with his psychiatrist resulted in yet another increase in the antidepressant medication.

He continued his downhill slide. On February 24, 2017, Ted met once again with his psychiatrist. His symptoms of depression included irritability, feelings of helplessness, lack of interest in everything, guilt, and anxiety. Another depression medication was added to his treatment protocol.

In March, he met with another psychiatrist who subsequently confirmed his mental health disability and that it had significantly impacted his capacity to function at his job. The doctor attested to the severity of his mental health challenges having escalated.

In August 2017, Ted gave notice he would be retiring three years earlier than originally planned. He would initiate extended leave on February 8, 2018, and remain on leave until his retirement date of April 28, 2018.

In Ted's own words:

I have decided to retire 3 years earlier than I had planned, because I can no longer function in this unreasonable and unethical work environment due to the oppressive quantitative visit count metrics that are impeding my ability to provide quality care to veterans.

RCS District 1 Deputy Director Dale Willis made a clinical site visit to the Warwick, RI VET Center in September of 2017. During this visit he acknowledged that he consistently heard the same concerns regarding the increased productivity mandate from other VET Centers he had visited.

SPEAKING TRUTH TO POWER

On January 18, 2018, Ted sent an email to the RCS Chief Officer Mike Fisher and the RCS District 1 Director, Debra Moreno, and RCS District 1 Deputy Directors, Dale Willis and Allison Miller. He sent this email in response to RCS leadership failing to address these issues that had been brought to their attention numerous times during the previous year-and-a-half through the normal chain of command.

The three-page single spaced email detailed the inaction by management when made aware of the adverse effect the policy was having on clinicians and veterans. He went on to outline the ramifications of not only the top-down implementation of a failing policy, but also shot holes through the subsequent instructions and consequences to counselors that did not successfully employ the new protocol into their practices. He goes on to criticize management, illustrating their failure as leaders and then graciously provided them with a methodology for redeeming themselves and correcting course.

This email essentially paints a graphic picture of a bad policy, implemented by senior management without seeking input from those in the field that would be tasked with implementing the policy. Management then hunkered down and mandated a clinical performance metric effectively penalizing counselors for not adhering to the ill-advised numbers game. One comes away from this email with several thoughts: Management is oblivious and insensitive to the needs of the people it is supposed to serve; arrogance pervades the management team in their not taking the slightest interest in righting the wrong; counselors and clients are not a priority.

It is very clear The Promise is no longer the mainstay of the VA VET Center program.

On January 25th, after not having received a response from any of the addressees on the January 18th email, Ted sent an email to the RCS Chief Officer, all RCS District Directors, all VET Center Directors and all RCS Counselors throughout the RCS system in an attempt to initiate an open conversation about these matters which were adversely affecting the veterans and counselors in the nationwide program. This email also included the one he had sent on January 18th.

From: Blickwedel, Ted W..
Sent: Thursday, January 25, 2018 12:24 PM
To: RCS Deputy Directors; RCS District Directors; VHA 10RCS Action; VHA RCS District 1 Vet Center Directors; VHA RCS District 1 Zone 2 Counselors; VHA RCS District 1 Zone 3 Counselors; VHA RCS District 1 Zone 4 Counselors; VHA RCS District 1 Zone 1 Counselors; VHA RCS District 2 Zone 1 Counselors; VHA RCS District 2 Zone 1 Vet Center Directors; VHA RCS District 2 Zone 2 Counselors; VHA RCS District 2 Zone 2 Vet Center Directors; VHA RCS District 3 Counselors; VHA RCS District 3 Vet Center Directors; VHA RCS District 4 Counselors; VHA RCS District 4 Vet Center Directors; VHA RCS District 5 Counselors; VHA RCS District 5 Vet Center Directors
Subject: CHANGE NEEDED IN RCS QUANTITATIVE CLINICAL PERFORMANCE EXPECTATIONS
To All RCS Counselors & Therapists,

On January 18th I sent the message enclosed below to the RCS Chief regarding the negative impact that quantitative clinical performance expectations have had on RCS clinicians (i.e. stress, health, morale, burnout, etc.). This issue has already been addressed through the proper chain of command by a number of VET Centers in District 1, Zone 1; especially during the past several months and longer in some cases. However, the leadership has not responded to these concerns; which is imperative for the care and support of RCS counselors and therapists, as well as their ability under this current duress to continue being able to provide quality counseling and therapeutic services to our veterans at an optimal level. Consequently, since this does not appear to be getting resolved after going through the appropriate channels, I have decided on my own accord to further illuminate this issue in an open forum to all concerned in the hope that everyone at all levels can work together to rectify this in a positive and compassionate manner.

The correspondence to the RCS Chief below describes the issue in more detail and offers suggestions on how to remedy this. I also encourage you to express any concerns and provide any constructive solutions you might have to your VET Center Directors, Deputy and District Directors, and the RCS Chief if this is relevant to your experience. Hopefully, this will be addressed by the leadership so there can be a healthy balance between quantitative measures at a reasonable level and the welfare of clinical staff.

Sincerely,

Ted Blickwedel, LICSW
Providence VET Center
2038 Warwick Avenue
Warwick, RI 02889
401-739-0167

From: Blickwedel, Ted W..
Sent: Thursday, January 18, 2018 4:46 PM
To: Fisher, Michael (1ORCS)
Cc: Moreno, Debra M.; Willis, Dale W.; Miller, Allison B.; Fortin, Rochelle LICSW, BCD; Furtado, Bernadette; DiCandia, Clarisse G..; Tarducci, Heather L.; Curran, James P; Santilli, Paul A.; Sherman, Jeanne M.; Medina, Jose; Witherell, Holly
Subject: FEEDBACK ON RCS CLINICAL PROCEDURES

Mike,

I am a retired Marine and combat veteran who has worked as a counselor at the Providence VET Center in Warwick, RI since January 2009. I have decided to retire early from RCS since the bureaucracy has degraded the ability of clinicians to properly perform their duties as counselors and therapists, which has negatively impacted the morale and welfare of VET Center staff. These concerns were addressed by our staff to Dale Willis who conducted a clinical site visit at our VET Center in September 2017. *Dale even acknowledged that he consistently heard the same concerns from other VET Centers he had been to. So, this is something that is a widespread problem and not limited to just a handful of employees.* However, it appears that none of the issues discussed have been attended to, which is critical for the well-being of clinical staff and ultimately the veterans we are here to serve. Consequently, I would like to offer feedback about this, as well as suggestions on how this might be resolved.

The biggest issue is productivity expectations for counselors. It used to be 50% for overall productivity and 40% for direct service. This seemed to be a reasonable number; especially considering the time that is necessary for consultation, progress notes, treatment plans, assessments, dealing with emergencies and crises, ROI correspondence, and other administrative duties. Subsequently, a few years ago, the expectation increased to 60% and 50% respectively which was feasible, but pushing the upper limit. However, **when the visit count number was added to the production expectation (86%-100% in percentage terms), that is when the difficulty for clinicians really began,** *especially due to the threats of negative action being taken for those who did not meet these expectations.* Not only was it not possible for some counselors to attain, it has come at great cost for those that have. I personally have struggled on a number of levels because of this, and have witnessed my peers' frustration and burnout. *Some clinicians have even started a medication protocol to cope with their anxiety.*

This has resulted in an ethical dilemma with having to choose between focusing on the numbers the leadership wants or providing quality services to our veterans which we are

53

primarily here for. These expectations force us to schedule appointments back to back on the hour every hour, having to account for cancelations and no-shows, which does not allow for adequate time to perform other duties mentioned above that are also expected. Further, **this is not conducive to conducting appropriate trauma treatment that often requires 80-90 minute sessions to properly execute.** _**Ultimately, the veterans suffer since they cannot be given the best care they deserve under these circumstances.**_

This is compounded by the leadership continuing to increase our administrative duties that often times is redundant and unnecessary (i.e. reconciling RCS visits against appointment schedules, adding more content to closing notes that is already contained in previous progress notes, filling out an extra checklist in the course of doing record audits when this information is already available in the electronic audit, etc.). So, we are either counselors or administrators. We cannot do both to extremes. **There needs to be a _healthy balance_.** Someone seriously needs to rectify this.

Additionally, there is the issue of taking care of our clinical staff, which is deplorable. Counselors have been and continue to be negatively impacted by what has been previously described. All we see is lip service being given to this by the leadership without any action. We predominantly only hear about numbers, numbers, numbers, production, production, production; and hardly anything regarding quality services, cutting edge trauma treatment, self-care, etc. The only person I have seen try to do anything about this is Allison Miller who is the Associate District Director – Counseling for District 1, Zone 1. She coordinated and conducted a self-care seminar via the tele-conference network for clinical staff approximately a year-and-a-half ago because of concerns she had about the well-being of counselors. Also, **it is amazing after the national Team Leader (Director) conference in Washington about two-and-a-half years ago that nothing has been done about the care and well-being of clinical staff from an institutional standpoint;** _**especially since there were apparently numerous accounts of VET Center Team Leaders during the conference who expressed**_ _**being depressed, and some with suicidal ideation**_**. Overall, this sends a message that the leadership does not care about RCS staff. It is both _unacceptable_ and _negligent_, and needs to be resolved for the sake of all concerned.**

I am sure the leadership genuinely wants RCS to provide the best possible services to our veterans. However, it appears the priorities are currently misguided and backwards since there seems to be more emphasis on servicing the bureaucracy rather than the veterans and staff. I know you and the rest of the leadership are dealing with organizational politics and mandates which are most likely shaping the decisions you have to make. Part of the problem is that we at the lower echelons are not privy to what is driving RCS policies and guidelines, which gives us the appearance when left in a vacuum that the leadership is incompetent because of decisions which are made that are contrary to the common sense of what is needed to effectively perform our clinical functions while taking care of RCS counselors. **We desperately need a course correction to fix all this, in order to enhance the well-being of clinical staff so they can provide optimal care for the veterans who deserve the best services we can give them.**

What I have explained here is also the opinion of the vast majority of RCS counselors I work with and who I know in other VET Centers. Many of them are reluctant to voice their concerns about this due to a fear of adverse repercussions they might experience if they do so. I personally have lost faith in the system and its leadership at this juncture, and consequently, have decided that it is in my best interest to retire and possibly be involved in this line of work in another venue that truly fosters an environment where one can provide the best PTSD-related trauma treatment, and that actually demonstrates a sincere interest in the self-care of counselors. Hopefully, for all my colleagues and the veterans that RCS serves, the leadership will wake up and do what is necessary to appropriately resolve this situation. Otherwise, they have failed their clinicians and the veterans they are here to help.

I thought long and hard about who I should include on this correspondence; especially since these concerns have been brought up before, but have apparently fallen on deaf ears without any response or resolution. Enough is Enough. The time for action is NOW. I have considered addressing this with Secretary Shulkin himself, as well as going to the media and/or sending this to all RCS Employees. I have not yet ruled that out, depending on how the RCS leadership handles this. However, I have decided for the time being to give you the benefit of the doubt. So, I will be watching, waiting and listening to see how this goes.

In conclusion, I recommend the following suggestions be considered by RCS to rectify these issues:

1. Modify the performance expectations to a reasonable level in order to minimize the stress of clinical staff and maximize their "quality" performance (i.e. eliminate or reduce the visit count to a feasible amount, go back to 50% for overall production & 40% for direct service).

2. Have more emphasis on the care and well-being of clinical staff, to include creating a committee if needed to establish guidelines to ensure this is occurring. This could even include half or full day retreats for clinical staff on or off site at determined intervals.

3. Advocating for necessary appropriations to fund adequate training for counselors, which had significantly declined a few years ago. This also includes granting AA to attend training, which has become more difficult over the last 3-4 years. None of this should be contingent on "quantity" of performance for liability reasons, as well as to enhance the professional development of all clinicians which ultimately benefits the veterans we serve.

4. Get feedback from the field before implementing any new policies or procedures which might adversely affect clinical services or the well-being of clinical staff. This would help optimize clinical performance and enhance the health and welfare of RCS counselors. Further, it will empower everyone to be vested and have a voice in the decision process which will boost morale.

5. In the future, hire only managerial staff at the District Level and above who have a clinical background and adequate clinical experience within the RCS system, in order to preserve the proper VET Center culture and to ensure appropriate clinical functions can be performed which are not impeded by someone without a clinical background who might establish policies that have a negative impact on clinical operations.

Sincerely,

Ted Blickwedel, LICSW
Providence VET Center
2038 Warwick Avenue
Warwick, RI 02889
401-739-0167

Mike Fisher responded immediately after Ted's second email struck a nerve. Fisher's response appears to have illustrated no real interest in taking concrete action to address the issues and rectify the situation.

From: Fisher, Michael (10RCS)
Sent: Friday, January 26, 2018 1:00 PM
To: Blickwedel, Ted W..; RCS Deputy Directors; RCS District Directors ; VHA 10RCS Action; VHA RCS District 1 Vet Center Directors; VHA RCS District 1 Zone 2 Counselors; VHA RCS District 1 Zone 3 Counselors; VHA RCS District 1 Zone 4 Counse-lors ; VHA RCS District 1 Zone 1 Counselors; VHA RCS District 2 Zone 1 Counselors ; VHA RCS District 2 Zone 1 Vet Center Directors; VHA RCS District 2 Zone 2 Counse lors; VHA RCS District 2 Zone 2 Vet Center Directors; VHA RCS District 3 Counselors; VHA RCS District 3 Vet Center Directors ; VHA RCS District 4 Counselors; VHA RCS District 4 Vet Center Directors; VHA RCS District 5 Counselors; VHA RCS District 5 Vet Center Directors
Cc: VHA 10RCS Action
Subject: RE: CHANGE NEEDED IN RCS QUANTITATIVE CLJNICAL PERFORMANCE EXPECTATIONS

You bring up an important point in that we all need to find more ways to talk to each other, bring up and discuss issues, and most importantly find solutions. This was the one of the main reasons why we started and are continuing with National Virtual Town hall meetings every month where staff can ask any question they want. Data and productivity questions do come up every time I meet with Vet Center staff. It is something that I believe will always be evolving as we try new things, interpret data in different ways, or the environment of Veteran's need changes. I recognize that there is concerns over productivity and we need to improve how we explain the standards and why these standards exist. We will start with getting rid of the color coding and find new ways to discuss the how and why behind these standards as we continue to review for improvements. We learned all too well in Phoenix several years ago the problems that can occur when policies are implemented without having a grasp on the capacity of an organization. We must all do our best to ensure nothing similar ever occurs in RCS.

Also brought up in the letter was training. I agree that is this a priority that we cannot ignore. At the beginning of the fiscal year, we required all Districts to develop face to face training opportunities for all positions to be ready to implement when the final budget is approved by the President. We also required the Districts to increase training through technology (VTel, etc.). While we believe that we will get an increase in the final budget for FY18 we cannot bank on that and need to prepare for a possibility of not receiving additional funding. With that in mind, we have asked all Districts to tighten the belt and only spend money on things that are absolutely required so we can focus resources to training staff.

Moving forward, email is not the best way of continuing this conversation and this conversation must continue. RCS Leadership is currently setting up a National Readjustment Counseling Service VAPulse page. We will send out the login information for everyone to join in the next week and will continue this discussion. I look forward to hearing your continued thoughts on VAPulse.

Thank you for the message and most importantly thank you all for what you do every day for Veterans, Service members, and their families.

Michael Fisher Chief Officer
Readjustment Counseling Service (10RCS)
202-461-6525
202-495-6206 Fax
Michael.fisher6@va.gov

Ted's response to the disingenuous email from Fisher is a *shot across the bow* and a *how dare you!* Ted was commanding the *waters be parted!*

Blickwedel, Ted W.

From: Blickwedel, Ted W.
Sent: Friday, January 26, 2018 3:06 PM
To: Fisher, Michael (10RCS); RCS Deputy Directors; RCS District Directors; VHA 10RCS Action ; VHA RCS District 1 Vet Center Directors; VHA RCS District 1 Zone 2 Counselors; VHA RCS District 1 Zone 3 Counselors; VHA RCS District 1 Zone 4 Counselors; VHA RCS District 1 Zone 1 Counselors; VHA RCS District 2 Zone 1 Counselors; VHA RCS District 2 Zone 1 Vet Center Directors; VHA RCS District 2 Zone 2 Counselors; VHA RCS District 2 Zone 2 Vet Center Directors; VHA RCS District 3 Counselors; VHA RCS District 3 Vet Center Directors; VHA RCS District 4 Counselors; VHA RCS District 4 Vet Center
Cc: Directors; VHA RCS District 5 Counselors; VHA RCS District 5 Vet Center Directors VHA 10RCS Action
Subject: RE: CHANGE NEEDED IN RCS QUANTITATIVE CLINICAL PERFORMANCE EXPECTATIONS

Mike,

In all due respect email is one of the best ways to continue this conversation. Not everyone is able be involved in town hall meetings and conference calls because of their over demanding schedules, which is driven by the expectation to meet the RCS clinical production numbers that is burning out counselors and therapists. I have already received a multitude of responses from clinical staff all over the country who are stressed out and hurting on a number of levels due the productivity level expectations. It is unreasonable and unrealistic for clinicians to continue operating like this and still be able to stay healthy and have the adequate time they need to provide the best quality services that our veterans deserve. I was literally in tears when reading some of the responses I received regarding how RCS counselors are being effected by the extreme duress they are experiencing because of the productivity standards (i.e. FMLA leave, depression, burn out, medication protocols, looking for other employment, retiring early, etc.). So, I don't think you really understand the magnitude of this problem.

The production expectations need to change or else clinical staff are going to continue being adversely impacted which will ultimately result in our veterans not getting the kind of quality care they should. So, as you mentioned, "improving how we explain the standards and why these standards exist" or "finding new ways to discuss the how any why behind these standards" is not going to resolve this issue. Further, you indicated below about "the problems that can occur when policies are implemented without having a grasp on the capacity of an organization, and that we must do our best to ensure nothing similar ever occurs in RCS". Well, it is already happening in RCS due to the new productivity and administrative standards and policies that have been promulgated over the last couple years, which has negatively impacted RCS counselors the way it has.

Additionally, the feedback I am getting so far also indicates that clinical staff feels that the leadership does not care about them and their well-being because of all this, and that their concerns are not being genuinely addressed. Whoever is coming up with these production standards is seriously out of touch with what is happening in the field and how it is adversely impacting those of us who are doing the day today therapeutic work. Consequently, there needs to be more than just talk about this. There needs to be action to make the actual changes that are necessary for the sake of RCS counselors and their well-being, which will give them the capacity to carry out the RCS mission at an optimal level. The bottom line is the productivity expectations need to be reduced to a fair and reasonable level so this can be accomplished.

I strongly encourage everyone to speak up and respond "reply all" with your comments so your voices are heard. The enormity of this issue and its impact needs to be fully understand by all. This won't happen if we don't share our concerns. This is a perfect opportunity to do so. Everyone needs to truly come together, both staff and leadership, so we can finally get real solutions. Hopefully, this will occur soon so this matter does not have to be elevated to the next level.

Sincerely,

Ted Blickwedel, LICSW
Providence VET Center
2038 Warwick Avenue
Warwick , RI 02889
401-739-0167

Dale Willis responded on behalf of Mike Fisher:

Blickwedel, Ted W.

From: Willis, Dale W.
Sent: Friday, January 26, 2018 5:40 PM
To: Blickwedel, Ted W.
Cc: Fisher, Michael (10RCS); Moreno, Debra M.; Fortin, Rochelle UCSW, BCD
Subject: RE: CHANGE NEEDED IN RCS QUANTITATIVE CLINICAL PERFORMANCE EXPECTATIONS

Ted: as we had discussed on our call with you please respect the chain of command. You are to cease and desist this email chain communication and follow the instructions of Mr. Fisher and continue the conversation on the VA Pulse link which will be provided next week.

Thank you

This was just the beginning.

Ted summarized what followed:

> I had received email responses and/or phone calls from 57
> different counselors from 42 VET Centers across 25 states who
> all conveyed that they and other clinicians at their centers have
> been negatively impacted by the clinical visit count expectations,
> which has degraded their ability to provide quality services to
> veterans (i.e., excessive stress, burnout, poor morale, health
> issues, depression, having to go on a medication protocol and/
> or seeing a therapist, time out of work, retiring early, looking
> for another job, etc.). In separate phone conversations I had
> with each of these counselors, most of them said they were
> afraid to speak up because of adverse repercussions they might
> experience, to include the possibility of losing their job.

THE SURVEY

On Saturday, January 27, 2018, Ted sent out a 5-point Likert Scale Survey
with 11 questions to all 1,300 (approx.) RCS counselors across the nation.

Blickwedel, Ted W.

From: Blickwedel , Ted W.
Sent: Saturday, January 27, 2018 7:56 PM
To: VHA RCS District 1 Zone 1 Counselors ; VHA RCS District 1
Zone 2 Counselors; VHA RCS District 1 Zone 3 Counselors; VHA
RCS District 1 Zone 4 Counselors; VHA RCS District 2 Zone 1
Counselors; VHA RCS District 2 Zone 2 Counselors; VHA RCS
District 3 Counselors; VHA RCS District 4 Counselors; VHA RCS
District 5 Counselors
Subject: RCS CLINICAL PRODUCTIVITY STANDARD IMPACT SURVEY

Attachments: RCS CLINICAL PRODUCTIVITY STANDARD IMPACT SURVEY.docx

To All RCS Counselors,

The attachment contains a RCS Clinical Productivity Standard Impact Survey. It is a short 11-question survey to rate the impact that the required clinical visit count is having on RCS counselors. It is critical that there is maximum input so this data can be collated for the purpose of presenting it to "appropriate entities" who can then better understand the concerns of clinical staff, in order to more strongly influence the proper resolution of this issue.

I know many of you are worried about the repercussions of expressing your opinion to the leadership. Consequently, this 5-point Likert Scale questionnaire is **completely anonymous**. All you have to do is circle your answer, include the date, and indicate your district and zone number.

There is only one person collecting these statistics. **So, please designate a counselor in your VET Center to collect the surveys and send them back to me in ONE attachment via email after they have been scanned into ONE document**. It viii make it much easier this way since there are over 300 VET Centers. Time is of the essence for a number of reasons. Subsequently, please have them sent back to me **no later than February 6th** if possible.

The more response we have the greater our voices will be heard. Otherwise, if we have limited input it may not be enough to effect the change that is necessary. This is our window of opportunity. It may not come again. Therefore, *I encourage you to respond so we can get the results that are needed*.

Ted Blickwedel, LICSW
Providence VET Center
2038 Warwick Avenue
Warwick, RI 02889
401-739-0167

RCS CLINICAL PRODUCTIVITY STANDARD IMPACT SURVEY

District #: _____

Zone#: _____   Date: _____

	Strongly Disagree	Disagree	Neutral	Agree	Stongly Agree
The current productivity standard for number of clinical visits required has caused me to be under significant duress in the workplace?	1	2	3	4	5
The current productivity standard for number of clinical visits required has negatively affected my health and well-being (i.e. increased stress, depression, anxiety, burnout, somatic symptoms, etc.)?	1	2	3	4	5
The current productivity standard for number of clinical visits required has caused me to seek therapy or go on a medication protocol?	1	2	3	4	5
The current productivity standard for number of clinical visits required has negatively affected my morale?	1	2	3	4	5
The current productivity standard for number of clinical visits required has degraded the quality of care I am able to provide to veterans?	1	2	3	4	5
The current productivity standard for number of clinical visits required does not allow me adequate time to complete mandatory administrative tasks (i.e. progress notes, treatment plans, assessments, ROI correspondence, etc.)?	1	2	3	4	5
The current productivity standard for number of clinical visits required has caused me to make a decision to leave the VET Center earlier than expected (i.e. look for another job, retire early, etc.)?	1	2	3	4	5
If I have not yet made a decision to leave the VET Center, I have considered it due to the current productivity standard for number of clinical visits required?	1	2	3	4	5
The current productivity standard for number of clinical visits required needs to be reduced to a reasonable level?	1	2	3	4	5
Only managers and directors with a clinical background should make policy decisions pertaining to clinical roles and functions?	1	2	3	4	5
I feel the leadership does not care about me and the well-being of other clinical staff?	1	2	3	4	5

Additional Comments:

Notably, this survey was sent out on a Saturday. Since most employees do not check their work emails over the weekend the response was muted. 27 counselors responded.

On Monday, January 29, 2018, RCS leadership had Ted's computer access terminated.

All administrative tasks and charting notes on clients were completed on computers. Computer access was integral to accomplishing job-related duties.

He was informed he was to use pen and paper to conduct business, including writing case notes on his clients.

Not entirely shot down:

In Ted's Chronology of Events, he states:

Even though this is not a large enough sample to establish statistical significance in an organization that has over 1,300 counselors, it still has some merit since the results of the survey were consistent with comments made by clinicians I spoke with who did not do the survey. They mentioned that they and their colleagues clearly felt the same as what was reflected in the survey. So, there is an obvious trend here that could not be fully exposed due to the RCS leadership not permitting the survey to be completed by telling counselors not to submit it, while disabling my computer access so I could not receive the input. Therefore, it should be noted what the questionnaire did uncover:

RCS CLINICAL PRODUCTIVITY STANDARD IMPACT SURVEY

Summary

Total Surveys: 27 (District #1: 12, District #2: 9,
District #3: 1, District #4: 3, District #5: 2)

Strongly Disagree = 1, Disagree = 2, Neutral = 3,
Agree = 4, Stongly Agree = 5

	Strongly Disagree	Disagree	Neutral	Agree	Stongly Agree
The current productivity standard for number of clinical visits required has caused me to be under significant duress in the workplace?	0	1	3	15 (56%)	8 (30%)
The current productivity standard for number of clinical visits required has negatively affected my health and well-being (i.e. increased stress, depression, anxiety, burnout, somatic symptoms, etc.)?	0	1	4	12 (44%)	10 (37%)
The current productivity standard for number of clinical visits required has caused me to seek therapy or go on a medication protocol?	4	5	3	7 (26%)	8 (30%)
The current productivity standard for number of clinical visits required has negatively affected my morale?	0	0	2	11 (41%)	14 (52%)
The current productivity standard for number of clinical visits required has degraded the quality of care I am able to provide to veterans?	1	0	3	10 (37%)	13 (48%)
The current productivity standard for number of clinical visits required does not allow me adequate time to complete mandatory administrative tasks (i.e. progress notes, treatment plans, assessments, ROI correspondence, etc.)?	0	1	1	4 (15%)	21 (78%)
The current productivity standard for number of clinical visits required has caused me to make a decision to leave the VET Center earlier than expected (i.e. look for another job, retire early, etc.)?	1	3	8	9 (33%)	6 (22%)
If I have not yet made a decision to leave the VET Center, I have conside red it due to the current productivity standard for number of clinical visits required?	1	2	2	15 (56%)	6 (22%)
The current productivity standard for number of clinical visits required needs to be reduced to a reasonable level?	0	0	0	7 (26%)	20 (74%)
Only managers and directors with a clinical background should make policy decisions pertaining to clinical roles and functions?	0	0	1	3 (11%)	23 (85%)
I feel the leadership does not care about me and the well-being of other clinical staff?	0	0	2	4 (15%)	21 (78%)

Notes

- 81% of counselors surveyed say that the visit count mandate has negatively affected their health & well-being.

- 85% indicated that it has adversely impacted their ability to provide quality care to veterans.

- 93% conveyed that the visit count mandate does not allow them enough time to complete administrative tasks.

- 93% expressed that the visit count mandate has negatively impacted their morale.

- 55% revealed that they have made a decision to leave the VET Center because of the visit count mandate.

- 96% disclosed that only directors with a clinical background should make policy decisions about clinical matters.

- 93% of counselors feel that the RCS leadership does not care about their well-being

- 100% of counselors surveyed voiced that visit count mandate needs to be reduced to a fair and reasonable level.

The survey results, limited in numbers as they are, should have at the very least provided a wake-up call for management.

That turned out not to be the case.

On Monday, January 29, 2018, Debra Moreno, District 1 Director, North Atlantic District, sent an email, reading in part:

It has come to my attention that you may have received a non-sanctioned email containing a survey over the weekend. Being non-sanctioned, this survey was not vetted, and you are in no way required to respond. In light of the recent discussions regarding the perceived productivity and administrative burdens being placed on the counselors, I ask you not to invest time and energy into this survey tool provided it will not be used by RCS Leadership in decision making.

She went on in the email to mention *VA Pulse*, an online site that serves to facilitate information sharing and promotion of new ideas. In many counselors' opinions, the *VA Pulse* was the *graveyard* for new ideas or anything that would be construed by management as input that was not in lockstep with their policy and agenda.

CHAPTER 7

Retaliation Tactics & Its Impact

R etaliation usually implies a payback of injury in exact kind, often vengefully. As seen on Merriam-Webster.com, it is defined as "to return like for like, especially to get revenge."

Recent Examples on the Web

- As part of the settlement, Amazon pledges not to retaliate against employees who discuss unionization outside of work facilities or on their own time.

    —NBC News, 23 Dec. 2021

- Facebook's global head of safety, Antigone Davis, told senators last week that her company wouldn't retaliate against the individual who provided senators with internal company research but stopped short of committing to wider immunity.

    —Laura Kusisto, WSJ, 5 Oct. 2021

- During a congressional hearing last week, lawmakers pressed Facebook global head of safety, Antigone Davis, not to retaliate against Haugen.

—Jessica Guynn, USA TODAY, 4 Oct. 2021

Whistleblowers find themselves in a unique situation. Whistleblowing is, by definition, calling attention to wrongs perpetrated on individuals, the government, or the private sector. Those individuals and/or organizations often retaliate for purposes of revenge and to protect themselves.

West's Encyclopedia of American Law, edition 2. (2008) defines whistleblowing as "The disclosure by a person, usually an employee in a government agency or private enterprise, to the public or those in authority, of mismanagement, corruption, illegality, or some other wrongdoing."

Whistleblowers experiencing retaliation are often personally, emotionally, physically and professionally devastated. This, too, usually has a severe negative impact on their families.

Jacqueline Garrick, LCSW-C, SHRM-CP, Founder and CEO of Whistleblowers of America, and Martina Buck, PHD co-authored an article, *Whistleblower Retaliation Checklist: A New Instrument for Identifying Retaliatory Tactics and Their Psychological Impacts After an Employee Discloses Workplace Wrongdoing.* This editorial analyzed the

Whistleblower Retaliation Checklist (WRC) survey results, hundreds of peer support conversations with whistleblowers, and it offers a comprehensive literature review.

The following are excerpts taken from the document:

[W]hen whistleblowers take on powerful, entrenched systems whose leadership has perpetrated or condoned these injustices, retaliation, harassment, and discrimination often ensues. These workplace traumatic stressors have long-term psychosocial impacts on these ethical individuals.

Yet, leadership within the organization vested in covering up the wrongdoing will use toxic and unethical tactics against the whistleblower who then suffers the psychosocial consequences. These tactics are a form of interpersonal violence that is created by a corruption of the institutional and ethical standards in order to exclude the whistleblower and minimize the culpability and damage to those responsible within the institution.

The authors dive deeper into the ramifications of retaliation:

Whistleblower Retaliation Stress risks are found to have a detrimental impact on employees' physical, mental, and social health status as they are designed to stigmatize, discredit, intimidate, and silence the whistleblower and are not only toxic to the individual, but to the organizational culture, coworkers, and the client base that the institution serves.

Initially, whistleblowers were discredited, often referred to as being disloyal, malcontents, dishonest, informers, snitches, one pejorative following another. Indeed, there are quarters that still refer to whistleblowers in this vein.

Conversely, increased numbers of people are more deductive in their reasoning as it pertains to whistleblowers and the value they bring to society. In many instances, some have been acclaimed as heroic, honest, courageous, and a credit to society.

Notwithstanding, the retaliation continues, as evidenced in the following excerpt taken from the "Whistleblower Retaliation Checklist (WRC)" illuminating responses from an open-ended survey polling whistleblowers on workplace wrongdoing as it pertains to retaliation:

> For WRC respondents, *the wrongdoing happened directly to them 79.4% of the time, 15% witnessed it, and 5.5% learned about it.* In describing "the worst event at work" most acknowledged one or more of the following themes: Being terminated, demoted, undermined, humiliated before peers or ruined reputation, harassed, bullied, alienated, isolated, falsely accused, privacy violated, threatened or emotionally abused, assaulted, injured or victimization/harm to others, arrested, and/or suicidal. These themes were consistent with other research that found that workplace bullying and (non-sexual) harassment could lead to PTSD.

If 70.4 percent of the whistleblowers have directly experienced retaliation in the workplace, alarm bells should sound. The problem is systemic.

Examples of retaliation tactics highlighted in the "Whistleblower Retaliation Checklist (WRC):"

1 GASLIGHTING: A term made famous by the 1944 movie, *Gaslight*, in which the abuser tries to convince his wife that she is mad through the flickering of a gas-powered lamp. Gaslighting is defined as the manipulation by psychological means of an individual in order to cause the subject(s) to question their own memory, perception, and sanity and is often associated with bullies, sociopaths, narcissists, and emotional abusers who want to deflect their own wrongdoing and belittle or degrade the intelligence of their victims and undermine their credibility as witnesses.

In the workplace, employees are scrutinized and challenged over disclosure details and complex laws, taunted as overreacting or misguided while the related wrongdoing is minimized or rationalized by their superiors or even the individuals investigating the allegations.

2 MOBBING: Occurs when management directly or indirectly pressures other employees to collude against and inform on the activities of the whistleblower. This includes monitoring their time and attendance, expenses, performance, or other issues and report any infractions.

3 MARGINALIZING: When whistleblowers are physically moved to minor assignments, relocated to a remote or an inferior location, or detailed to nominal projects not commensurate with their job description, which then enables Devaluing.

4 SHUNNING: Where marginalizing physically isolates and publicly humiliates employees, *Shunning* ostracizes or socially alienates them from their team or other emotionally supportive colleagues. It thwarts their sense of belongingness, purpose, and meaning, which are factors often associated with depression and suicide.

5 DEVALUING: The following set of indicators were designed to evaluate *Devaluation* of the employee. When performance ratings

are unexpectedly lowered; benefits denied; promotions, bonuses or awards are missed; being demoted or training opportunities are lost; then the employee is suffering Devaluation. This is often inconsistent with past performance appraisals and ignores previous awards and recognitions.

6 DOUBLE-BINDING: Is associated with mixed messages and contradictions usually from someone of greater power (a parent, spouse, or a boss) to manipulate the mental status of the victim. Although, it may seem like a chance for redemption to the employee post whistleblowing, Doubling-Binding is a tactic that gives the worker a new set of seemingly important tasks, but with insufficient resources or unrealistic deadlines. If the whistleblower fails to deliver, then their performance is penalized (Devalued), or if successful, then credit is diverted, or plagiarism is sanctioned.

7 BLACK-BALLING: Occurs when a whistleblower tries to move to another office, division, corporation or field of practice, but their professional reputation has been so ruined that it hinders their ability to obtain substantial gainful employment.

8 COUNTER-ACCUSING: Once identified, whistleblowers may experience *Counter-Accusations* that impugns their credibility and assassinates their character as an honest broker of events. Mobbing is used to help build a complaint against the whistleblower and charges trumped up against them are investigated and documented—usually involving their performance or accountability. This not only holds the whistleblower to a different standard than a similar group of employees, it can ultimately result in their termination or resignation (under hostile circumstances this is known as constructive dismissal).

On follow up interviews through WoA, two whistleblowers recounted being arrested because their employer (Department of Veterans Affairs Medical Centers) filed charges against them that were later dropped as severe intimidation.

9   EMOTIONAL and PHYSICAL VIOLENCE: Employees report being emotionally, physically, and sexually harassed or abused, threatened, bullied, or cyberbullied, including their families (Interagency Security Committee, 2013) in attempts to cover up or shut down their allegations. For WRC indicators related to *Emotional and Physical Violence*, there was evidence that employees felt confronted or threatened at some level 88.7 percent of the time and harassed 99 percent of the time. Ninety-four percent had been bullied in a way that left them fearful while 75 percent worried about their physical safety. Consistent with Federal Bureau of Investigation data, 14 percent had been physically or sexually assaulted. Because of their disclosures, 15.3 percent had family members who were also targeted or bullied.

Other points of interest, as it relates to the impact of retaliation, were gleaned from the "Whistleblower Retaliation Checklist (WRC)":

• Survey results validate that toxic management tactics correlate to serious psychosocial impacts on whistleblowing employees and their workplace environment. The WRC confirms that retaliation threatens a worker's sense of safety, security, trust, belongingness, purposefulness, future, self-esteem, and ability to self-actualize, which further impairs their psychological and physical health and infiltrates their family and social network.

• Whistleblowers may suffer from negative self-esteem, anger at injustice, confusion about legal processes, loss of trust, remain horrified by the harm caused, become disinterested in previously satisfying or enjoyable activities while ruminating about the wrongdoing and their complaint, and feel a growing detachment and estrangement from others. Hypervigilance and exaggerated startle response are reported particularly among those who have experienced threats of violence, (cyber)bullying, and other forms of harassment. Furthermore, those stigmatized by their leadership are also more likely to suffer from these symptoms.

Other examples of whistleblower retaliation strategies:

1   Termination

2   Suspension

3   Demotion

4   Reassignment of duties

5   Reduction or denial of benefits

6   Denial of bonuses

7   Ridicule

8   Isolation

9   Punishing

In Ted's own words he describes the whistleblower retaliation tactics used against him by VA/RCS/VET Center management:

> During this advocacy process to address the adverse impact that the excessive productivity expectations were having on counselor welfare and quality care, I discovered that the reprisal tactics I experienced by VA/RCS management were the usual strategies they and other government bureaucracies employ to silence those who speak truth to power, in order to avoid accountability for their negligent guidelines, policies and regulations which have harmful effects on employees, or people receiving services. At first, as I was encountering this retaliation, I did not fully realize what was happening. However, I knew something was wrong and it did not feel right. Later, I became aware that this retribution was an

orchestrated effort by VA/RCS management to suppress my discourse since it compromised their agenda, and that there are actual terms to describe this castigatory approach when dealing with individuals who voice their concerns which are controversial.

The first of these toxic tactics I experienced was *shunning*. This started at my last staff meeting on January 31, 2018, when my VET Center Director, Rochelle Fortin, agreed beforehand that I could address the staff at the meeting in order to have closure with my colleagues due to my near-term departure, subsequent to the emails and survey I had sent to all RCS counselors throughout the system. During our gathering, while trying to facilitate completion with my peers, Rochelle interrupted and accused me of violating the chain of command which was not relevant to the dialogue since I was attempting to say farewell to my coworkers and express my gratitude for our relationship. This intrusion created a negative tone for the conversation that made staff members uncomfortable, which did not allow for a proper completion while running out of time to do so. Another opportunity to accomplish this was never granted by Rochelle when she refused to be part of my retirement celebration a few months later that was organized by 2 fellow counselors. This caused a couple other counselors at the VET Center to not be part of it due to fear of possible consequences from Rochelle, because of giving the appearance it would be supporting me after she tried to turn the staff against me through making misleading comments to them which falsely insinuated that I was dangerous and a threat.

These disingenuous remarks Rochelle made about me were at a staff meeting on February 7, 2018, approximately 6 days after I had gone on terminal leave prior to my official retirement date. I was told by 2 VET Center staff members later that day that Rochelle said the following at different times during the meeting: "When I came into work this morning I was looking around since I thought Ted could be lurking somewhere nearby," "Ted knows where we all live," "Ted is very precise and calculating."

Further, one of these staff members also conveyed to me that on another day, Rochelle stated, "I thought Ted's office was locked when he left. I wouldn't be surprised if he made extra keys before he departed." Additionally, these same two staff members acknowledged this as witnesses in an Interrogatory that was submitted for my EEO complaint against Rochelle. They indicated, in their opinion, that Rochelle was trying to further distance me from her and the staff by perpetuating unfounded notions about me that had no basis in fact. They further agreed that she was doing this because of being afraid of how my communication about the issues I was addressing with RCS leadership and VET Center counselors across the country would reflect on her if she did not cooperate with VA/RCS management in trying to silence my voice and taint my character and credibility. They said, too, there are a few staff members who do not trust her after observing how she unfairly treated me without just cause, in order to protect herself at my expense.

Counteraccusations were also fabricated against me at the end of January 2018 and during February 2018, which have been continued since then. Initially, I was told that I violated the chain of command by sending emails to my colleagues to address the adverse effect that the excessive productivity expectations were having on counselor welfare and quality care. In fact, this is not the case for reasons I previously described.

Further, the RCS District 1 Deputy Director, Dale Willis, accused me via email on February 27, 2018, that I *pressured* my VET Center Director, Rochelle Fortin, when she called me at home on February 22, 2018, since he stated that I insisted on coming to the VET Center, which is not true. In the VA response to the Interrogatory for my formal EEO complaint, Rochelle also claimed that I forced a conversation with her by attempting to call her multiple times and asking her to join me for lunch. This, too, is fictitious.

Additionally, I was wrongly accused by Dale Willis in an email on February 23 & 27, 2018, that my behavior created a high level of anxiety for staff members and that the police would be called if I ever showed up at the VET Center. I did not do anything inappropriate to deserve this negative and unjust treatment, since l never committed any acts of aggression, hostility, or threatening behavior towards anyone. This can be verified by two of my peers who have supported me through this entire process. Consequently, this action by Dale and Rochelle was a conniving and malicious attempt to manipulate the optics of this situation to blame me for causing a distressing environment, when it was actually generated by the way they falsely portrayed me as being a danger or threat to instill irrational fears in my colleagues with no basis in fact so they could further isolate me from them and the rest of the staff. This unwarranted and deceitful spin on their part also served them in trying to silence me and avoid accountability for their own improper conduct. As one of my coworker's stated in emails dated February 23 and March 1, 2018, "this angers me for you" and is "ridiculous" and "insane." They are "the real threat, not you." Their endeavor to physically isolate me from the VET Center and staff is another whistleblower retaliation tactic called *marginalizing*.

Another retaliation tactic I encountered was *mobbing*. This occurred within a few months after I left the VET Center when Matt Killoran, RCS District 1 Associate Deputy Director, met individually with counselors during a visit to the VET Center where I used to work. According to a couple of my peers, he attempted to convince them that all the allegations I claimed about the adverse impact of clinical productivity expectations were not real and in my head. These same colleagues told me they felt intimidated by this and believed that Matt was trying to destroy my credibility and turn everyone against me by making them think I was misguided, overreacting, and crazy. This *mobbing* strategy also applies to the *shunning* comments Rochelle made to other employees at the staff meeting on February 7, 2018, in order to compel them to be afraid of me through her misleading remarks by implying that I was threatening and dangerous.

Further, I experienced *gaslighting* in a public forum, numerous times, through the VA's response to my media interviews which were broadcast on local and national levels. They constantly side-stepped the issue being addressed as if it did not exist, and then used clinical performance statistics to deceptively justify why their productivity expectations were not a problem, while completely ignoring evidence-based research and feedback from VET Center counselors to the contrary. This deflection and manipulation by VA/RCS management was deceiving and very misleading to avoid accountability for their own wrongdoing, as well as to belittle and degrade my intelligence and integrity.

On March 22, 2021, I was informed that a No Trespass Order was filed against me after I stopped by the VET Center on March 9th to drop off a memorial donation for a former counselor who recently passed away. Two of my peers who work at the VET Center notified me that the staff received an email from Rochelle Fortin which stated she was going to have a No Trespass Order issued against me because I had no business being at the VET Center, even though I was following instructions in the deceased's obituary that donations could be given for veterans at the VET Center in her memory with Rochelle as the point of contact. It should be noted that Rochelle was not at the VET Center the day I delivered my donation. She decided to take this unwarranted action on baseless grounds, which further was vicious and spiteful under the circumstances, according to my colleagues who warned me about the forthcoming No Trespass Order. So, this is just another incident of VA/RCS management trying to *shun, intimidate* and *marginalize* me, even though it is underserved.

On June 28, 2021, as a result of credible evidence and documentation forwarded to the Warwick Police Chief by a law firm I hired, the Warwick Police Department decided to revoke the No Trespass Order, since it was determined that the accusations Rochelle made against me were blatantly false and very misleading (e.g., implying that I am a mentally unstable combat veteran, etc.). At no time was I a danger to anyone at the Vet Center, nor did I ever threaten anyone there. These whistleblower retaliation tactics I was subjected to, and its impact on me, are well substantiated in the interrogatories of two coworkers who had the courage to support me in my EEO complaint with the Office of Resolution Management (ORM). Also, this is documented in emails from these same colleagues, to include emails they sent to the lead Government Accountability Office (GAO) investigator whose team conducted an inquiry into my claims regarding the excessive and unreasonable productivity standards.

Ted goes on to reveal the impact retaliation had on himself, his family, peers and clients:

> The psychosocial impact of these reprisals was extensive and severe. On a personal level, it was devastating to my health and well-being, legally stressful, and financially burdensome. My family, peers, and clients, too, were seriously affected by this.
>
> Initially, I was only stunned and moderately upset by the *shunning, counteraccusations,* and *marginalizing.* However, as the original shock wore off, I felt deeply hurt, disrespected, and rejected by not being allowed to have proper closure with my coworkers. As the retaliation progressed, and I became more aware of how this was an orchestrated effort to discredit and silence me, I experienced feelings of isolation, loneliness, invalidation, humiliation, worthlessness, betrayal, anger, rage, and profound distress. This triggered my service-connected depression which gradually escalated into despair with borderline suicidal ideation. I then isolated at home in February and March 2018 and was very sedentary while being consumed with filing all my grievances and complaints with various federal agencies (i.e., OIG, OSC, & ORM).
>
> As a result of this inactivity, combined with my grave emotional state during this timeframe, I suffered from a submassive pulmonary saddle embolism on March 31, 2018, which should have killed me. I was in the Intensive Care Unit (ICU) for 4 days between the Providence VA Medical Center and RI Hospital.
>
> Destructive emotions lingered for months and were accompanied by insomnia, irritability, and a sense of hopelessness. This was compounded by the *mobbing* and *gaslighting* I previously described. The *gaslighting,* too, prompted me to have some

self-doubt about my sanity and perception regarding the allegations I was promoting. Further, my reputation was ruined in some circles within the VA/RCS, to include among some of my colleagues at the Warwick, RI VET Center who were turned against me by the unscrupulous reprisal tactics employed by VA/VET Center Program management. Also, most RCS counselors who backed me on the side in other VET Centers across the country gradually stopped communication with me, which left me feeling even more abandoned at times.

The cascading effect from these distressing events severely eroded my sense of belonging and caused me to lose any sight of having meaning or purpose. At this juncture, around June 2018, I was at a place of complete desperation and realized I had to take care of myself if I was going to get through this, which I had neglected up to this point since I was consumed and overwhelmed by the demeaning and ruthless retaliation while trying to move forward with my advocacy efforts. Consequently, in July 2018, I participated in a week-long therapeutic intensive which helped me to navigate through and partially heal from the impact of this trauma. Afterwards, as needed, I used various relaxation and grounding techniques to maintain a healthy mental, emotional, and spiritual balance.

There were also legal and monetary repercussions that resulted from this. I incurred almost $10,000.00 in legal expenses to be represented by an attorney during my informal EEO mediation process, which was financially difficult. This was compounded by accumulating another $24,000.00 in legal fees to get the baseless No Trespass Order against me rescinded, as well as to pursue an ethics violation complaint with the RI Department of Health Licensing Board against my former director at the Warwick VET Center.

Besides the damaging effect these reprisals had on me, my family and coworkers were also adversely impacted. My wife and adult children felt isolated and cutoff from me due to my tendency to be withdrawn since I was emotionally disconnected and unavailable most of the time. Occasionally, I even avoided family functions or would sometimes disappear at social events to be by myself. Although my wife and I were able to have decent and effective communication, our intimate relations declined significantly because of my emotional distance.

My colleagues at the Warwick, RI VET Center were negatively affected due to their heightened anxiety through witnessing the callous retaliation I received from VA/RCS management, especially two of my peers who supported me throughout this entire process. Most of them were scared to have contact with me since they were afraid of potential reprisals against them if they did, or because some of them might have bought into Ms. Fortin's dishonest attempt to depict me as being dangerous or some kind of threat. Further, a few of my coworkers were angry due to the unfair and cruel treatment I was given, as well as upset since they were not able to have proper closure with me upon my departure from the VET Center. This has caused ongoing divisiveness among the staff, to include mistrust of Ms. Fortin and upper management within the VET Center Program. Two of the colleagues who have defended me think they could be the next targets, and one of them, in February 2022 left the VET Center for another position because of the toxic work environment and not feeling safe. Also, clinicians from VET Centers in other parts of the nation conveyed to me that they have retired early, obtained jobs outside of the VA, or gone into private practice due to experiencing or witnessing unethical and harmful retaliation practices by RCS management, as well as because of the excessive productivity standards.

Unfortunately, too, some of my astute veteran clients picked up on what was happening before I retired, since they noticed the tense atmosphere at the VET Center and told me they heard from other sources what was going on. Some of them were very upset and said they would never come back to the VET Center after I left. I was also informed by RCS counselors in other states that they had clients who could see the shift in tone at their VET Centers due to the increased pressure clinicians were feeling because of the excessive productivity standards and additional administrative burdens being placed on them. Further, these counselors conveyed to me that some of their clients were aware of reprisals occurring against clinicians for expressing their concerns about the harmful production metrics, which caused some of these clients to stop participating in services within the VET Center Program.

The overall adverse impact of the unreasonable productivity expectations and the outrage resulting from the reprisals I and other counselors encountered is what initially strengthened my resolve and to continue addressing these issues and seek corrective action due to my strong sense of fairness and justice. My motivation to take this on was greatly enhanced on January 26, 2018, as I broke down crying in my office when reading the overwhelming replies to my nationwide emails from counselors all over the country who shared their stories about how their health, well-being, and morale had been seriously harmed by the excessive production standards and the retaliation they witnessed against those who voiced their concerns. It was apparent in their responses that they had a glimmer of optimism that VA/RCS management might actually rectify these problems since it was now out in the open and in the forefront. In this moment, I felt responsible to advocate for this cause as far as I could go, since I realized I had opened Pandora's Box by inciting some hope that *maybe* the VET Center Program leadership would remedy this situation.

Of course, as has already been explained, the traumatic effect of the cumulative mistreatment I experienced took a heavy toll on me, and because of it I admittedly almost gave up my advocacy endeavor a number of times.

However, what inspired me to keep this campaign going was twofold:

- The success I had along the way with raising awareness regarding this dispute through local, state, and national news coverage of interviews I had done with various media organizations.

- Gaining the support of my US Congressional Delegates in RI who initiated a Government Accountability Office (GAO) investigation which eventually substantiated my allegations.

CHAPTER 8

No Trespass Incident

Note to reader: The matter concerning No Trespass is written in a manner not unlike a police report to vividly illustrate how Ted learned he could trust no one in upper management within the VA. This also elucidates how the Warwick Police Department did not follow its own policies, thus favoring the powerful VA.

Wednesday, March 9, 2021: Three years after retiring from the VA, Blickwedel arrived at the Warwick, RI VET Center to drop off a memorial donation on behalf of a former colleague, Barbara Feeley, who had recently passed away, in accordance with the instructions in her obituary.

The Center was open, but the doors were locked.

A woman with whom Blickwedel was not familiar came to the door, and asked Blickwedel how she could be of assistance.

Blickwedel asked to see the director, Rochelle Fortin, as he had something he wanted to give to her.

He was informed by the acting office manager, Kim Walker, that he would not be allowed inside due to COVID, and that Ms. Fortin had not come into work that day.

Blickwedel gave the donation to Ms. Walker to give to Ms. Fortin.

Blickwedel then inquired, mentioning some of his former associates, if he could speak with any of them.

Jeanne Sherman, learning that Blickwedel was standing outside the VET Center entrance went outside to speak with him.

Blickwedel also spoke with Chris Morse outside the front entrance to the VET Center. Mr. Morse had also worked with Barbara Feeley prior to her retirement in 2010. As Blickwedel was a pall bearer, Mr. Morse expressed interest in her funeral arrangements.

Blickwedel remained outside of the Warwick VET Center facility for the duration of his visit.

Ms. Feeley's obituary specifically requested that the donation, per the deceased's wishes, be used for veterans who receive services at the Warwick VET Center.

Blickwedel departed the VET Center without incident.

Tuesday, March 16, 2021: VET Center Director Rochelle Fortin contacted the VA Police Department. She was directed to reach out to the Warwick Police Department.

Wednesday, March 17, 2021: Cpl. Steven Cileli and Cpl. Randy Botelho from the VA Police went to the Warwick VET Center and took a report from Rochelle Fortin.

Cpl. Botelho and Cpl. Cileli then responded to the Warwick Police Department and spoke with Officer Bruce Law, explaining the incident to him. Officer Law stated he would file a report and start the process to notify Mr. Blickwedel of a No Trespass Order being placed on him by their department.

Ms. Fortin was advised to contact all her employees regarding Blickwedel not being allowed on the property and to contact the Warwick Police immediately if he arrives at that location.

Tuesday, March 21, 2021: Officer Bruce Law of the Warwick Police Department wrote the following in a police report:

> Based on Blickwedel's behavior, it was determined that Cileli wished to have him Trespassed from the facility. I was able to contact Blickwedel via telephone. I spoke with Blickwedel and informed him of the no trespass order, and I advised him that if he returned to the facility, he would be arrested. He stated he understood the terms.

Months later, Blickwedel received a copy of the March 17th and March 21st VA and Warwick Police reports.

During an interview conducted with Blickwedel and consistent with later accounts by his colleagues, his response to Fortin's complaint is summarized below:

1 When I went to the Vet Center to deliver the donation, I never demanded entry or bullied anyone as Fortin claimed.

2 She falsely asserted I had no right or business to be at the center, when I was legitimately there to drop off a memorial donation according to the wishes of the deceased stated in her obituary.

3 She stated I was convinced to leave without incident, which is not true. In fact, two of my former colleagues came out to talk with me. If they had been concerned that I should not be there, they would have told me so or notified the police. They did not. They were interested in speaking with me. It was a congenial visit.

4   She stated the employees were afraid of me because I had been presumed to have brought a gun to the VET Center. The report states there was no evidence or proof that I had brought a gun to the center. No one said they were concerned that I had brought a gun there at any time.

5   I never demanded that she provide a reference letter as she insisted when I was in the process of getting a weapons permit.

6   I never bragged to anyone that I had a concealed weapons permit as she stipulated. However, a few close co-workers were aware I had a permit during the course of casual conversation. Also, I never made the statement to anyone that "No one would ever know I was carrying a weapon."

7   I was not hostile at work or make employees feel uncomfortable as she said. Occasionally, I expressed my frustrations with associates, but in the same manner everyone else did at times.

8   Ms. Fortin also falsely insinuated I had regular sudden outbursts.

9   I never locked myself in my office as she claimed. However, I did close the door when meeting with clients for privacy. I also kept my door cracked open when I was alone so staff members could knock and enter when they needed to see me.

10   I absolutely never stood at attention outside my office for long periods of time as Ms. Fortin insisted. This is clearly her attempt to paint me as a mentally unstable combat veteran to justify her unwarranted mistreatment of me.

11   She untruthfully claimed in the report I was offered EAP/Counseling. However, she did suggest that I should attend to my own self-care.

12   Ms. Fortin's version of events that occurred in her office are not true. I never made the statement "You are against me and aligned with the

district." What I did say was, "I don't trust you anymore. You demonstrated poor leadership by the way you conducted the staff meeting where I was trying to have closure when you interrupted me and made false accusations against me as I was speaking to team members."

13 She claimed in the report that when I placed my hand in my pocket, she thought I was going to pull out a gun and that she was going to die. In fact, she recounts how I pulled out a set of keys and placed them on her desk. In this instance, she was intentionally creating a false narrative to validate her retaliation agenda, to include obtaining a No Trespass Order against me.

14 She stated that I had reached out to many of the employees at the VET Center to convince her to have closure with me. This is totally untrue. What actually happened was I requested Dale Willis, RCS District 1 Deputy Director, to arrange a reconciliation meeting with me and Ms. Fortin, with Dale being present at that meeting. The purpose was to bring an end to the acts of reprisal being directed against me by her and upper management.

It should be noted that neither the VA Police nor the Warwick Police Department spoke with Blickwedel or any of his former co-workers prior to the No Trespass Order being issued.

In an interview conducted when writing this book, Blickwedel said in part:

So, they're going off and creating this narrative, making it appear as if I'm threatening or a mentally unstable veteran. This is their fallback position behind the scenes, to try to justify why I was essentially banned from the VET Center and saying that the police would be called if I came there. I have emails, you know, that state this very thing from Dale Willis. And you know, that is just nonsense.

Jeanne Sherman, who spoke with Ted the day he dropped off the memorial donation at the VET Center, was interviewed by Ted's attorney about that encounter. Here is a synopsis of what she said during the interview that refutes Fortin's account in the police report:

- She had a very cordial conversation with Ted at the front entrance of the VET Center.

- She said Ted never entered the building and that he did not insist to come in.

- She felt comfortable with Ted, had a lot of respect for him, considered him a mentor, and that he had a good working relationship with all his colleagues.

- She never felt intimidated by Ted and did not ever see him standing at attention outside the door to his office.

- She never observed anything that was strange about Ted's behavior.

- She never recalled Ted saying anything about firearms that concerned her in any way.

- She did not remember any co-worker ever saying that they were concerned about Ted or that they were intimidated by him.

- She stated that VA supervisors were not happy that Ted went to the press.

- She also was worried and frustrated about the implementation of the new productivity standards, and that the VA was losing site of providing meaningful mental health services to veterans. She thought this would negatively affect the quality of care they receive. Because of this, she decided to retire on December 31, 2021.

Included below are verbatim excerpts from a Report of Contact (in Lieu of VA Form 119) that was taken from two of Blickwedel's associates regarding another employee at the Warwick VET Center, Jose Medina. Blickwedel was mentioned by name in this interview. These excerpts are included to further illustrate Fortin's modus operandi as Director of the Warwick VA Center:

> This is an example of a tendency toward favoritism that Rochelle Fortin exhibits toward some members of her staff and not others. In this context, Rochelle Fortin has written up Jose Medina about conflicts to which more than one staff member contributed, but she did not write up others. She has also written up Jose Medina claiming he was dangerous and someone who made staff members feel intimidated. This appears to me to be a pattern of defamation of character.

The following are verbatim excerpts from an interrogatory with one of Blickwedel's female associates vis-à-vis an EEO complaint filed by Blickwedel:

Some staff (usually the female administrative/program assistants) displayed similar behaviors, and they were not confronted or reprimanded. Her response was (Fortin) often excusing and supporting them. Her accusations were also exaggerations and/or distortions.

> I believe sex was a factor because as a male, he can easily be accused of being hostile, intimidating and threatening, thereby creating an uncomfortable environment. In addition, office manager Jose Medina, who is male, was also falsely accused of being hostile, threatening and creating an uncomfortable environment.

> Not at all. I never seen or heard Ted do or say anything that would indicate harming anyone.

Please note that the Complainant is Ted Blickwedel.

Yes, I think that the fact that the Complainant is male, and he may be seen as possibly intimidating by Ms. Fortin may be the reason that she made these allegations about C (complainant).

I will repeat the part that is most relevant to this question: Given that Ms. Fortin already knew that the Complainant had a military service-connected disability, the Complainant told me that he felt he was being provoked to have some sort of negative episode that would give them (Ms. Fortin and Mr. Willis) recourse to say that they were right in their negative allegations about the Complainant. There are no grounds that I can think of that would lead me to believe that the Complainant would ever be less than professional. The fact that he was accused of forcing a conversation with his supervisor or creating an uncomfortable environment in any way seems preposterous to me. It is just not the Complainant I know that would do any such thing as what he was accused of doing. He is about harmony and creating win/win resolution to problems.

It is important to note the following, which occurred on or about February 23, 2018. This verbatim interrogatory was obtained from the same EEO complaint:

Complainant was restricted from the VET Center without clearing it first with Dale Willis, Deputy Director, District 1 (e.g., three years prior to Blickwedel's attempt to drop off the memorial donation he had left at the VET Center).

Did you receive an email, forwarded by the Complainant, that was originally sent from Dale Wills to the Complainant on February 23, 2018, which said the Complainant is not to go to the Vet Center without calling him (Dale Willis) first?

Response: Yes.

To your knowledge, why did Dale Willis place this restriction on the Complainant?

Response:

In my opinion the Complainant did not do anything to warrant or justify the restriction. As I have stated before in various contexts in the Interrogatory, there is nothing that I have ever learned or witnessed about the Complainant that would make me anxious to have him show up in our VET Center or anywhere else in my life. The anxiety noted in the email is completely unjustified in my opinion.

Monday, March 22, 2021 – Blickwedel wrote a letter to the VA requesting a copy of the VA Police Report.

Tuesday, March 23, 2021—Richard Rowe, VA FOIA/Privacy Officer, wrote a letter to Blickwedel, stating in part:

My review of the documents revealed that they fall withing the disclosure protections of FOIA Exemption 7, 5 U.S.C. 552(b) (7)(A). Exemption 7(a) permits VA to withhold a document or information in a document if the agency compiled the document for a law enforcement purpose and if disclosure of the information could be reasonably expected to interfere with law enforcement proceedings. The VA Police have advised me that this case is still under investigation. Therefore, I must withhold the police report in full.

Thursday, April 1, 2021—Blickwedel hired a legal firm, Pannone, Lopes, Devereaux & O'Gara LLC (PLD&O), to get the No Trespass Order rescinded.

Friday, April 23, 2021—Attorney William P. Devereaux of PLD&O wrote a letter to Michael Ursillo of the law firm of Ursillo, Tietz, & Ritch, Ltd. (UT & R), solicitors for the City of Warwick, Rhode Island. The letter detailed prior events relating to the issuance of the No Trespass Order, and requested that it be rescinded.

In this letter, Devereaux noted:

> The Providence Veterans Center office is a public space and is paid for by taxpayer dollars. Ms. Fortin nor anyone else at that location or Mr. Cileli has a private ownership on that property.
>
> Blickwedel was entitled to due process prior to (and certainly after) the issuance of this notice. As you know, Rhode Island has a criminal statute governing "willful" trespass … which essentially provides that a notice of trespass must be issued prior to citing a person with a criminal misdemeanor violation of the law. Public building and grounds present a bit more complicated issue and while Rhode Island has no cases directly on point, caselaw does exist indicating that a person has a right of due process before being subjected to a no trespass notice to a public venue which could potentially lead to criminal charges. The principle that an individual possesses a liberty interest in remaining in a public place of his or her choosing is well established. At minimum, due process requires notice and an opportunity to be heard to "be granted at a meaningful time and in a meaningful manner." Due process is ordinarily absent if a party is deprived of his or her property or liberty without evidence having been offered against him or her in accordance with established rule. Even if it is impractical for the City to provide a pre-warning hearing to assure that there are reasonable grounds to support the trespass warning, the City must provide some post-deprivation procedure to satisfy the element of the Due Process Clause.

It is recommended the reader refer to the letter for additional insight and clarity as to its content (*www.VAbreakingpromises.com*).

Devereaux ended his letter with the following paragraph:

> Here a representative of the VA presented vague allegations against LTCOL Blickwedel to the Warwick Police referring to undefined behavior during his visit to a public office. There is no indication that the officer ever followed up with any inquiry regarding the specifics of what exactly this individual was alleging that Ted Blickwedel did – other than attempting to enter his former place of employment and indicating he had something to give to Ms. Fortin. Hence there is no substantive basis for the issuance of this trespass warning barring him for some unknown period from entering a public space. Finally, my client was, and is, entitled to due process which includes his right to challenge this order if it is not rescinded. Unfortunately, the motivation for seeking this trespass notice appears to relate more to personal animosity towards LTCOL Blickwedel by certain VA personnel. LTCOL Blickwedel would rather not pursue legal action against the City of Warwick regarding this specific issue and hope that the matter can be resolved at this level. Based upon the foregoing, I hope that you can notify me that the City will rescind this Notice of Trespass forthwith.

Thursday, June 3, 2021 – Attorney Devereaux wrote a second letter to Michael Ursillo. This letter says in part:

> I write as a follow up to my letter to you of April 23rd, 2021, and the conversations we have had since your receipt of my correspondence. You also forwarded to me another police report that was initially withheld from Mr. Blickwedel which essentially

contained a detailed statement from Mr. Blickwedel's former supervisor, Rochelle Fortin. I note at the outset that this entire report is based upon the version on one person – Ms. Fortin. I am presenting you with sworn statement of other witnesses/ employees of the Vet Center (attachments A&B), taken before my involvement in this matter and prior to the alleged incident of March 9th which led to the issuance of this "No Trespass Order". You will see that these documents present an entirely different picture of relevant events. Also included are written statements of these same VA employees on behalf of another veteran VA employee (attachments C&D) who experienced the same type of toxic treatment from Ms. Fortin. Also enclosed (as attachment E) is a copy of a Senate Bill submitted at the request of Senators Jack Reed (D-RI) and Jon Tester (D-MT) specifically targeting the VA's new productivity standards. This Bill addresses the very same questions that Ted Blickwedel had initially raised with his supervisors and was subsequently compelled to bring forward in a whistleblower status to the appropriate authorities.

Tuesday, June 29, 2021, 10:42:26 – Devereaux received an email from Ursillo, quoted in part below:

I've convinced the police department to drop the No Contact order for your client based on all the background information you provided.

Tuesday, June 29, 2021, 11:47:32 – Devereaux responded to Ursillo's email:

Mike; thanks for getting back to me. That is good news. Can you send me something on City letterhead that the "no trespass order" has been withdrawn? I am sure my client will want confirmation.

Tuesday, June 29, 2021, 11:50 AM – Devereaux sent the following email to Blickwedel:

> Ted: good news. The Chief is withdrawing the no trespass order. See below. However, also review my communication to Ursillo clarifying certain points and requesting follow up. I will reach out to you later today.

Tuesday, June 29, 2021, Colonel Bradford E. Connor, City of Warwick Chief of Police, wrote a letter on City letter head to Devereaux stating in part:

> Attorney Devereaux,
>
> This letter is in reference to Warwick Police Department report 21-1467-OF concerning your Client Theodore Blickwedel (dob X/XX/XX). The no trespass warning that was issued by Officer Bruce D. Law on behalf of The Department of Veterans Affairs Police Department on March 17, 2021, for the Vet Center at 2038 Warwick Ave has been withdrawn as of June 28, 2021.

Monday, September 20, 2021, Ted's attorney sent a letter to Rochelle Fortin. In this letter he informed her that the Warwick Police Department had rescinded the no trespass order. It said in part:

> The documents we submitted indicated that the information you provided to the VA Police Department, which they in turn provided to the Warwick PD, was either patently false and/or greatly exaggerated. At no time was Ted Blickwedel a threat to anyone at the VET Center nor is there any credible evidence that he had made any type of threats to any personnel who worked at the VET Center or any clients who visited the location.

Something that stands out is the premise that Ted visiting the VET Center is protected by law. The VA Police and the Warwick Police Department appear to have either intentionally disregarded this fact or are ignorant of the law. Neither of which is acceptable.

This September 20th letter lays it out:

> Furthermore, the Veteran's Center on Jefferson Boulevard in Warwick is a facility rented by the United States Government and anyone from the public, including Mr. Blickwedel, has a right to access that building for legitimate purposes.

Attorney Devereaux then addressed the core issue in his letter:

> We view the actions taken by you and the Veteran's Administration in this matter to constitute retaliation and harassment against Ted Blickwedel for actions he took to address what he believed, in good faith, was the institution of a client quota system which negatively impacted the level of care provided to our Veterans. Your action to date constitutes actionable defamation and harassment.

In an effort to achieve a modicum of accountability, Devereaux made a promise to Ms. Fortin:

> Furthermore, please be advised that if you, or anyone at the VA, engages in further harassment and retaliation, or publishes any defamatory claims designed to injure our client's reputation with the general public or within the VA system, we will seek any and all legal remedies against you and/or the Veteran's Administration as appropriate.

On September 20th, 2021, the letter sent by Devereaux to Fortin was copied to Michael Fisher, RCS Chief Officer, in Washington, DC. Fisher oversees the VET Center Program, which includes the Warwick, RI VET Center where Fortin is the director.

Ted, through his attorney, spoke Truth to Power. Truth won!

CHAPTER 9

Ethics

E thics is derived from the Greek words *ethos/ethikos* (character) and from the Latin word *mores* (customs).

Over the centuries, ethics has been defined as *"that which is good for the individual and how it is applied to society as a whole, tasking the individual to act in the interest of the common good."*

The National Association of Social Workers (NASW) is an organization made up of over 148,000 social workers. It was founded in 1955 by consolidating a host of organizations to include, but not limited to the American Association of Social Workers, American Association of Psychiatric Social Workers, American Association of Medical Social Workers, and the National Association of School Social Workers.

Social workers, as defined by the NASW, are "professionals devoted to helping people function the best they can in their environment."

The NASW has a far-reaching influence nationwide, to include all 50 states, the District of Columbia, Guam, the US Virgin Islands and Puerto Rico. *All of the beforementioned entities' licensing boards require their licensees adhere to the NASW Code of Ethics.*

All social workers must be licensed in the state(s) in which they practice.

Therefore, all social workers, be they counselors or social workers serving in management, are required to adhere to the NASW Code of Ethics.

Social workers are encouraged to become members of an NASW chapter in the state in which they are licensed to practice. Though membership is not required, adhering to the NASW Code of Ethics is essential when licensed.

All social workers and social work students, regardless of their professional functions, the setting in which they work, or the subpopulations they serve are legally bound to following the NASW Code of Ethics.

With this baseline in mind, it is imperative to note that all individual(s) highlighted in this book are required to follow guidelines outlined in the NASW Code of Ethics.

Social workers who are believed to have violated the Code of Ethics are to be reported to the licensing board in the state in which they practice and/or the local NASW chapter.

On January 19, 2022, Ted filed a complaint with the Rhode Island State Board of Social Work Examiners for Licensure of Social Workers. Ted's attorney's cover letter and Ted's complaint follow:

PANNONE LOPES DEVEREAUX & O' GARA LLC

Counselors at law
William P. Devereau

ETHICS

January 19, 2022

Ms. Laura Mello, Board Manager State Board of Social Work
Examiners for Licensure of Social Workers

Rhode Island Department of Health, Room 105A 3 Capitol Hill

Providence, RI 02908

Re: Complaint of Theodore Blickwedel

Dear Chairperson and Members of the Board:

I represent Theodore "Ted" Blickwedel who is a Licensed
Independent Clinical Social Worker (LICSW) in the State
of Rhode Island who worked for nine years at the Veteran
Administration's VET Center in Warwick, RI, where he conducted
individual and group therapy with combat veterans. Ted is also
a retired Marine and disabled combat veteran.

After significant consideration, and my review of the facts of
his case, Ted decided to file the enclosed complaint against his
former supervisor who is an LICSW and still the Director at the
VET Center. The complaint speaks for itself. However, I believe
it also illustrates a government dedicated more to numbers and
appearance than to providing substantive care to our veterans,
as well as a callous disregard of the NASW Code of Ethics which
involved unwarranted retaliation directed towards a dedicated
social worker because he addressed the detrimental impact that
agency clinical performance measures were having on mental
health services for veterans and counselor welfare.

The complaint is thoroughly documented. On behalf of Mr.
Blickwedel, it is our sincere hope that this matter will be given
the careful attention it deserves. Please do not hesitate to
contact me if you would like to speak with Mr. Blickwedel or any
other potential witnesses, or to obtain other relevant evidence.

Sincerely,

/s/William P. Devereaux
William P. Devereaux, Esq.
PANNONE LOPES DEVEREAUX & O'GARA LLC

January 14, 2022
Mr. Theodore Blickwedel
c/o William P. Devereaux, Esq.
Pannone Lopes Devereaux & O'Gara LLC
1301 Atwood Avenue, Suite 215N Johnston, RI 02919

The Board of Social Work Examiners for Licensure of Social
Workers Rhode Island Department of Health
3 Capitol Hill
Providence, RI 02908

**Re: Complaint of Theodore Blickwedel pursuant to Title 216,
Chapter 40, subchapter 05, Part 7.5.**

Dear Members of the Board:

Please accept this as my formal complaint against LICSW
ROCHELLE FORTIN. The pertinent facts supporting this
complaint are as follows:

1. I am a retired US Marine combat veteran and a licensed
   clinical social worker previously employed by the Veterans
   Administration (VA) at the Providence Veterans Center
   located at 2038 Warwick Ave., Warwick, R.I. I worked at
   the Vet Center providing counseling to fellow veterans for
   approximately nine years (2009-2018). I found my work at
   the Vet Center fulfilling and productive until approximately
   the last 2 1/2 years of my service there. In September
   2013, a fellow social worker and colleague, Rochelle Fortin,
   was appointed as the Director of the VET Center which
   employs approximately seven counselors. I always felt that
   I had an excellent working relationship with Ms. Fortin,
   and we were cordial to each other.

2. However, this relationship began to change when the VET
   Center Program management in Washington D.C. announced
   in 2016 that it was implementing new clinical productivity
   standards concerning the number of visits each counselor
   must see in a 40-hour work week. This directive from the
   VA in Washington D.C. mandated that each counselor must
   have 30 clinical visits per week, which essentially is a 50%

increase compared to what counselors were expected to achieve under the old system. Most of the counselors at the Center (and it was later learned, across the country) strongly felt that these arbitrarily imposed quotas would be detrimental to the quality of care and services they provide every day to our veterans. The amount of time a counselor provides to his/her clients varies depending on the severity of their conditions and their symptoms which is recognized by applicable professional standards. Despite the VA's preference to service larger numbers of veterans at its VET Centers, there simply is no "one size fits all" category. As a combat and disabled veteran, I felt I had a unique perspective that the trauma each veteran presents with is never exactly the same. I voiced my objection to the implementation of this system, and in January 2018, I submitted a written complaint to management and directors in the VET Center Program chain of command, which included my direct supervisor, Ms. Fortin. However, I never received a substantive response and as time went on it became clear to me that I was now viewed by Ms. Fortin and her regional superiors as a boat rocker and not a "team player." Nevertheless, I continued to press the position that these unilaterally imposed productivity metrics would continue to have a negative effect on counselor welfare and degrade their ability to provide the best possible care to veterans and their families. After receiving an insignificant response from the VA chain of command, I contacted my RI Congressional Delegates in March 2018 regarding this situation and was also interviewed numerous times by local and national news organizations between April 2018 and November 2021. During this process, I was made aware that Ms. Fortin had made comments to other colleagues depicting me as a troublemaker and inferring that I was mentally unstable (See sworn interrogatory responses of VET Center counselors: Dr. Clarisse DiCandia (PsyD) and Bernadette Furtado, LICSW (Exhibits A and B). Ironically, a Government Accountability Office (GAO) investigation of this matter, initiated by Senator Reed (D RI), substantiated my allegations in September 2020 (Exhibit **C)** and, further, that a hostile work environment existed at the Providence

Vet Center (Exhibits A and B). As a result of the GAO investigation, Senators Jack Reed (D-RI) and Jon Tester (D-MT) introduced legislation **(S. 1944)** to the Senate Committee on Veterans Affairs which specifically targets the VA's new productivity standards for scrutiny and addresses the very same issues that I had initially raised with my supervisors (Exhibit **D).**

Congressman Cicilline also sponsored the House version of the Senate Bill **(H.R. 3575)** and introduced it to the House Committee on Veterans Affairs. However, even though I have the support of my RI Congressional Delegates and the GAO who validated my claims, I continued to be shunned, rebuffed, and marginalized by Ms. Fortin and other VET Center Program management for addressing these concerns.

3. I believe my actions were in accord with the NASW Code of Ethics, in particular: **Section 2.03** Interdisciplinary Collaboration (Social workers for whom a team decision raises ethical concerns should attempt to resolve the disagreement through appropriate channels. If the disagreement cannot be resolved, social workers should pursue other avenues to address their concerns consistent with client well-being); **2.05 Consultation** (Social workers should seek the advice of colleagues whenever such a consultation is in the best interests of clients); **3.07** Administration (Social workers should advocate for resource allocation procedures that are open and fair. When not all clients' needs can be met, an allocation procedure should be developed that is nondiscriminatory and based on appropriate and consistently applied principles); **3.09** Commitments to Employers (Social workers should work to improve employing agencies' policies and procedures and the efficiency and effectiveness of their services); (Social workers should take reasonable steps to ensure that employers are aware of social workers' ethical obligations as set forth in the NASW Code of Ethics and of the implications of those obligations for social work practice); (Social workers should not allow an employing organization's policies, procedures, regulations, or administrative orders

108

to interfere with their ethical practice of social work. Social workers should take reasonable steps to ensure that their employing organizations' practices are consistent with the NASW Code of Ethics); **5.01** Integrity of the Profession (Social workers should work toward the maintenance and promotion of high standards of practice); (Social workers should uphold and advance the values, ethics, knowledge, and mission of the profession ...) **5.02** Evaluation and Research (Social workers should monitor and evaluate policies, the implementation of programs, and practice interventions); **6.04** Social and Political Action (Social workers should engage in social and political action that seeks to ensure that all people have equal access to the resources, employment, services, and opportunities they require to meet their basic human needs and to develop fully. Social workers should be aware of the impact of the political arena on practice and should advocate for changes in policy and legislation to improve social conditions in order to meet basic human needs and promote social justice).

4. As this Board knows, **R.I.G.L. 5-39.1-5 Agency Powers,** provides that "The Department of Health shall promulgate rules and regulations that may be reasonably necessary for the administration of this chapter and to further its purposes."

5. Title 216, Chapter 40, subchapter 05, entitled, "Professional Licensing", adopted pursuant to the above referenced statute, indicates in Section 7.2 that "These regulations adopt and incorporate the 'The NASW Code of Ethics (1999)' of the National Association of Social Workers by reference, not including any further additions or amendments thereof and only to the extent that the provisions therein are not inconsistent with these regulations."

6. As set forth in more detail below, Ms. Fortin willfully violated the Code of Ethics in her actions and conduct towards me and another Providence Vet Center employee, Jose Medina, who is also a veteran.

7. Unfortunately, I was not the only Providence Vet Center Employee singled out by Ms. Fortin for disparate treatment. Jose Medina, also a Marine Corps veteran, served for 27 years as an Office Manager at the Vet Center. Mr. Medina was good at his job and particular about following proper procedures. As described in the sworn statements of Dr. DiCandia and Ms. Furtado (LICSW), as well as in their reports of contact (ROC) (Exhibits E and F), Ms. Fortin began a campaign of criticism against Mr. Medina and targeted him for termination. Fed up with the toxic environment in the office, Mr. Medina also elected to retire.

8. Since it became clear to me that Fortin and VA supervisors were more interested in implementing the bureaucratic clinical production metrics than in finding a suitable alternative to ensure the protection and sustainment of veteran quality care and counselor welfare, I decided to retire from the VA three years earlier than I had contemplated. I advised Ms. Fortin and requested that I be allowed to address fellow counselors at the January 31, 2018, staff meeting for mutual closure of my career and to express my feelings on this and other issues. A "closure/farewell" at a staff meeting was standard practice at the Vet Center when a counselor was retiring or leaving. I indicated to Ms. Fortin that my intention was to be positive and constructive in my remarks. I was told that I would be allowed ample time to address my co-workers. However, during the staff meeting, Ms. Fortin waited until less than ten minutes remained on the schedule to allow me to speak. I was less than a couple minutes into my presentation when Fortin accused me of "not following the chain of command." It was clear that she did not want me to express what I had to say to her or our colleagues, most of whom I had worked with for many years. The meeting ended awkwardly, and I felt that I had been intentionally silenced. I also subsequently learned that Ms. Fortin continued to defame my reputation by inferring to my colleagues and others that I was mentally unstable, dangerous, and overly interested in firearms.

110

9. A review of Exhibits A, B, E, and F indicate that there was no credible basis for these statements and inferences. They are simply false.

10. Nevertheless, I retired from the VA with a retirement date effective on April 28, 2018, and had taken terminal leave prior to that which commenced on February 1, 2018.

11. Subsequent to my departure from the Vet Center, I never returned there for three years. In early March 2021, I learned that a much-beloved colleague I had worked with at the VET Center, Barbara Ann Feeley, had passed away. In her obituary (Exhibit G) **it** was stated that, "in lieu of flowers, donations in Barbara's memory may be made to the Veterans Center in Warwick, RI in care of Rochelle Fortin. Any donations made will be turned into gift cards for groceries, gas cards, etc. It would please Barbara so much for people to support the veterans of Rhode Island."

12. Following the directions outlined in Ms. Feeley's obituary, on March 9, 2021, I went to the Providence VET Center to provide a donation to Ms. Fortin in Barbara's memory. When I arrived there, I was greeted by a temporary female office manager who I had never met who told me I couldn't come inside due to the Covid protocol then in effect. I complied with her instructions. When I mentioned to her that I had a memorial donation to drop off to Rochelle, she informed me that Ms. Fortin was not present at the VET Center. I then handed her a labeled envelope with my donation inside, since she said she would place it on Rochelle's desk for me. I then asked her to see if any of my peers were available to come to the front door so I could speak with them. One of my former coworkers, Jeanne Sherman, then came up to the entrance and I spoke with her there for several minutes. Jeanne and I had a friendly and cordial conversation. Afterwards, I spoke with another colleague, Chris Morse, at the front door for approximately five minutes. Both Jeanne and Chris seemed genuinely happy to see me. Ms. Sherman, who later spoke with my attorney, Mr. Devereaux, indicated to him that she recalled I had mentioned the passing of Barbara Feeley and that I had

come to the VET Center that day to drop off a donation in her memory. She also stated to my attorney that we spoke outside of the doorway due to Covid protocols (Exhibit H). After I finished talking with Chris, I got into my vehicle and left. I later received a letter of thanks from Donna Russillo, Chief of Voluntary Service for the Providence VA Medical Center, for my donation in Barbara's memory (Exhibit I).

13. I was therefore stunned when on or about March 21, 2021, I received a phone call from a Warwick Police officer who advised me that the Warwick Police Chief had issued a "No Trespass Order" barring me from setting foot on the Providence VET Center premises, and that if I went there again, I would be arrested and criminally charged with trespassing. I was completely dumbfounded and immediately went to the Warwick Police Department to obtain a copy of the police report, but they only gave me a partial, redacted version which contained vague allegations (Exhibit J). Since I had been unilaterally barred from entering a public building based upon non-substantive, and what I believed were false allegations, I retained an attorney.

14. My attorney was able to obtain a redacted copy of the complete police report, which we then learned also included a report from the VA Police in Providence that contained statements made against me by Rochelle Fortin. These statements were outright falsehoods and contained complete exaggerations (Exhibit K). My attorney then wrote to the Warwick City Solicitor and included the sworn statements of Dr. DiCandia and Ms. Furtado (LICSW) which clearly refuted the statements made by Ms. Fortin (Exhibit L). My attorney, William Devereaux, of Pannone Lopes Devereaux & O'Gara LLC also requested that if the No Trespass Order was not rescinded that I be afforded a hearing which I was entitled to according to the R.I. Supreme Court. Mr. Devereaux sent the Warwick solicitor a follow up letter (Exhibit **M)** and ultimately the No Trespass Order was rescinded (Exhibit N). Unfortunately, I spent a significant amount of funds, which I had saved for retirement, for Mr. Devereaux's services. Further, I feel I have yet to recover

my good reputation which I had earned through my 27-year career in the Marine Corps and 9 years of service as an LICSW at the Providence VET Center counseling fellow veterans.

15. In summary, Ms. Fortin, a licensed clinical social worker and supervisor, continued her unwarranted retaliation against me by dishonestly using law enforcement to have me unjustly banned from the VET Center, a public building, which further stigmatized me and damaged my reputation as a social worker through her false and exaggerated statements and claims.

16. A relevant part of the NASW Code of Ethics states in its preamble that, "Value: Integrity. Ethical Principle: Social workers behave in a trustworthy manner. Social workers are continually aware of the profession's mission, values, ethical principles, and ethical standards and practice in a manner consistent with them. Social workers act honestly, responsibly, and promote ethical practices on the part of the organizations with which they are affiliated". Further, in the same preamble the Code states that its ethical standards are applicable to "social workers' ethical responsibilities to colleagues", and "social workers' ethical responsibilities as professionals."

17. Section 2 of the NASW Code of Ethics sets forth social workers ethical responsibilities to colleagues. Ms. Fortin's conduct in this case violates Sections 2.01 (a), (b), and (c); 2.03 (a); and 2.04 (a). Specifically, Ms. Fortin has violated these sections of the Code as follows:

a. 2.01 (a): Social workers shall treat colleagues with respect and should represent accurately and fairly the qualifications, views, and obligations of colleagues: *In her actions and conduct, Ms. Fortin clearly did not treat me with respect and did not accurately and fairly represent my qualifications, views and obligations. The sworn interrogatories, reports of contact, statements submitted by independent witnesses* (Exhibits A, B, E, F, and H), *and my own report of facts indicate that once I raised the*

113

issue of how the excessive clinical productivity standards unilaterally imposed by the VA were detrimental to quality mental health care for our veterans and counselor well-being, I was targeted and spoken about negatively by Ms. Fortin to other colleagues by portraying me as a mentally unstable social worker, fascinated with firearms, who was obsessive and compulsive, and inferentially a danger to my colleagues. This negative campaign continued when Ms. Fortin made a false and exaggerated complaint to law enforcement in an effort to obtain a "no trespass order" unilaterally barring me from visiting or entering my former place of employment and to further stigmatize me within the Providence Vet Center and within the VA health care system.

b.   2.01 (b): Social workers should avoid unwarranted negative criticism of colleagues in communications with clients or other professionals. Unwarranted negative criticism may include demeaning comments that refer to colleagues' level of competence or to individuals' attributes such as race, ethnicity, national origin, color, sex, sexual orientation, age, marital status, political belief, religion, and mental and physical disability: *In her actions and statements Ms. Fortin falsely portrayed me as a mentally unstable combat veteran who was a troublemaker and not a "team player." Her negative comments persisted when she made untruthful and exaggerated statements to law enforcement to physically bar me from visiting the Providence VET Center.*

c.   2.01 (c): Social workers should cooperate with social work colleagues and with colleagues of other professions, when such cooperation services the well-being of clients: *Ms. Fortin by her statements and conduct did not cooperate with me or others in seeking a resolution to these unilaterally mandated productivity expectations. On the contrary, she did everything to silence me and portray me as an unbalanced rabble rouser despite the opinions of other colleagues that these clinical productivity metrics would hamper the provision of quality care and counselor welfare. It appears Ms. Fortin's focus was on pleasing her superiors and to snuff out any complaints about mandating and enforcing an unethical program as attested to by other personnel.*

d. 2.03 (b): Social workers for whom a team decision raises ethical concerns should attempt to resolve the disagreement through appropriate channels. If the disagreement cannot be resolved, social workers should pursue other avenues to address their concerns consistent with client well-being: *Ms. Fortin knew that other social workers at the Providence VET Center had ethical issues with these newly enforced productivity standards. While at first, she did not complain about my or others' efforts to resolve these issues by registering our complaints up the chain of command, she then clearly sought to silence me when I communicated with other VA social workers across the country seeking to obtain their views on this new "system." I had received a myriad of comments from other colleagues stating their dissatisfaction with this "one size fits all" productivity system (Exhibit* **O).** *Ms. Fortin's response was to collude with senior VET Center Program management to have my computer account disabled so that I would be prevented from having further professional contact with colleagues on this issue. The other avenues I pursued were clearly frowned upon by Ms. Fortin and her superiors at the VA (contact with US Senators and Representatives, numerous interviews with local and national media organizations, etc.).*

e. 2.04 (a): Social workers should not take advantage of a dispute between a colleague and an employer to obtain a position or otherwise advance the social workers' own interests: *Ms. Fortin, by her actions and statements and her negative campaign against me, clearly wanted to demonstrate to her superiors that she was a "team player" as they defined it and had control of her office and the people she supervised. By marginalizing me and portraying me as mentally challenged and disruptive, she sought to advance her own interests during this dispute and never attempted to resolve it in a positive way.*

f.   2.11 (c): Social workers who believe that a colleague has acted unethically should seek resolution by discussing their concerns with the colleague when feasible and when such discussion is likely to be productive: *During my terminal leave period and prior to my official retirement date, I attempted to speak with Ms. Fortin and her Deputy District Director on several occasions to arrange a meeting with them regarding the retaliation tactics she and her superiors were using against me because I raised concerns about the enforcement of what I believed was an unethical productivity mandate that was focused on the number of veterans seen rather than counselor well-being and the quality of mental health care services provided. Essentially, I was rebuffed and ignored. When I was engaged in having mutual closure with my colleagues at the last staff meeting I attended, Ms. Fortin cut me off and accused me of "not following the chain of command" which I clearly had complied with. When I attempted to have a meeting in her office either one-on-one or with her supervisor present, she refused to meet indicating she needed time and space to digest what had happened (e.g., I still do not understand what she meant by that, but at any rate, she refused to meet with me). As a supervisor of social workers at the VET Center, Ms. Fortin should have been more than willing to meet with me to discuss these issues. Her refusal to do so is a violation of this section of the Code of Ethics.*

g.   3.01 (d): Social workers who provide supervision should evaluate supervisees performance in a manner that is fair and respectful: *The exhibits presented, and my recitation of facts indicate that due to my raising an ethical issue with the productivity system, Ms. Fortin sought to marginalize me with my colleagues and degrade my reputation by making statements to the effect that I was mentally unstable (i.e., that I had stood at attention outside my office for long periods of time); obsessive (i.e., that I knew how many steps there were between the VET Center and another building, and that I knew where they all lived); overly interested in firearms; and a person who disregarded the chain of command. She then treated me as if I was a threat to the VET Center and my colleagues by insinuating through her false accusations that I was dangerous and then by obtaining a "no trespass order" without cause from the Warwick Police Department by making untrue and exaggerated statements she provided to the VA police, knowing that the VA Police would present these statements to the Warwick Police.*

h. 3.07 (b): Social workers should advocate for resource allocation procedures that are open and fair. When not all clients' needs can be met, an allocation procedure should be developed that is nondiscriminatory and based on appropriate and consistently applied principles: *The evidence submitted establishes that the clinical productivity system implementation, which was adopted without input from counselors in the field, would negatively affect the provision of quality care to veteran clients. Rather than trying to advocate for a fair and equitable procedure, Ms. Fortin essentially adopted the productivity standards without question and expected clinicians at the VET Center to accept it. If anyone proposed that this system was detrimental and unethical (like I did), they were silenced and/or marginalized.*

i. 3.07 (d): Social Work administrators should take reasonable steps to ensure that the working environment for which they are responsible is consistent with and encourages compliance with the NASW Code of Ethics. Social work administrators should take reasonable steps to eliminate any conditions in their organizations that violate, interfere with, or discourage compliance with the Code: *It is clear that Ms. Fortin did not encourage compliance with the Code, but rather discouraged it by effectively retaliating against me in my efforts to adhere to the code, which also prevented other counselors from voicing their concerns due to fear of reprisals after witnessing her mistreatment of me.*

j. 3.09 (c): Social workers should take reasonable steps to ensure that employers are aware of social workers' ethical obligations as set forth in the NASW Code of Ethics and of the implications of those obligations for social work practice: *Ms. Fortin made no attempt that I am aware of to educate anyone in her chain of command about the Code and how the excessive productivity metrics would negatively affect compliance with the Code. When I consistently brought this subject to her and her superiors' attention, I was marginalized, gaslighted, and branded as dangerous and mentally unstable.*

k. 3.09 (d): Social workers should not allow an employing organization's policies, procedures, regulations, or administrative orders to interfere with their ethical practice of social work. Social workers should take reasonable steps to ensure that their employing organizations practices are consistent with the **NASW** Code of Ethics: *As a supervisor of social workers at the VET Center, Ms. Fortin had an obligation to not allow the unilateral application of the clinical productivity standards to interfere with the ethical practice of social work. She failed in her responsibility and singled me out for negative treatment when I consistently indicated that this system would not allow us to properly treat our clients.*

    Ultimately I retired three years earlier than I had planned, since I determined that I could not ethically participate in this system.

l. 4.04: Social workers should not participate in, condone, or be associated with dishonesty, fraud or deception: As stated herein and illustrated through the attached exhibits, Ms. Fortin was dishonest and deceptive in her statements to the VA Police and in the statements she made to others at the VET Center about me. Other colleagues have given sworn testimony concerning these misrepresentations which were designed to bar me from my former workplace, which is a public building, and expose me to criminal charges if I went there again. While it certainly was not and is not my intention to frequent the VET Center, this action was designed to malign my reputation in the social worker community and in the community in general. I was initially advised that my name was being placed in a file at the Warwick Police Station containing "active no trespass orders," until the Warwick Police Chief revoked this order because it was without merit since it was based on fraudulent statements made by Ms. Fortin about me.

m. 4.06 (a): Social workers should make clear distinctions between statements made and actions engaged in as a private individual and as a representative of the social work profession, a professional social work organization, or the social workers' employing agency: *Ms. Fortin violated this section of the Code because the false and exaggerated statements she made about me occurred in the workplace as a supervisor and to the VA police, as the supervisor of social workers at the VET Center. Her negative statements and characterizations were made while cloaked with the authority of a supervisor of that office.*

n. 4.06 (b): Social workers who speak on behalf of professional social work organizations should accurately represent the official and authorized positions of the organization: *Ms. Fortin violated this section of the Code by presenting false and inaccurate statements as the supervisor of the Providence VET Center to the VA police, also knowing that those statements would be presented by a VA police officer to the Warwick Police Department.*

In summary, I do not make this complaint lightly or without considerable thought. However, the actions taken, and the statements made against me by Ms. Fortin are clearly calculated, untrue, unjust, vindictive, and violate the NASW Code of Ethics. I certainly should not have had to defend myself by having to hire an attorney to rebut false and inaccurate statements made by Ms. Fortin to law enforcement to rescind a wrongfully issued no trespass order. Furthermore, I should not have been singled out for negative treatment and been the subject of unwarranted and damaging statements due to my raising legitimate ethical issues and by following the provisions of the NASW Code of Ethics. In section 2.11 (d), the Code instructs that, "When necessary, social workers who believe a colleague has acted unethically should take action through appropriate formal channels (such as contacting a state licensing board or regulatory body, an NASW committee on inquiry, or other professional ethics committees)." This is what I am doing. I also note that section 2.11 (e) of the Code indicates that, "Social workers should defend and assist colleagues who are unjustly charged with unethical conduct." I believe that is what colleagues like Dr. DiCandia, Ms. Furtado (LICSW), and others have done and are prepared to do in this case.

Respectfully submitted,

Theodore Blickwedel
Encl.

On January 24, 2022, Ms. Linda Julian, a Health Policy Analyst for the RIDOH sent a letter to Ted's attorney, which stated in part:

Mr. Blickwedel's complaint had been received by the Board; that investigating a case's merits *might take a long time*; that Mr. Blickwedel might be contacted for additional information or to clarify statements made in the complaint; and that if the matter proceeded to an administrative hearing, Mr. Blickwedel and other witnesses would likely be called to testify.

On February 2, 2022, Ted's attorney received correspondence from Ms. Laura K Mello, Public Health Promotion Specialist, Board Manager, Center for Professional Boards and Licensing. Excerpts from the one-page letter follow:

> The Rhode Island Department of Health (RIDOH) has completed a thorough review and investigation into the allegations made in your client's complaint dated January 19, 2022. RIDOH's investigations include a review of all materials provided by you, communications with the parties involved, and a comprehension of applicable Rhode Island law.

This statement was a blatant falsehood, as a thorough investigation could not have been conducted in a nine-day period nor had the complainant or four witnesses been contacted.

Ms. Mello's letter also directed Devereaux to the RIDOH to their website to ascertain the board's findings:

> [Y]ou will find such action posted on the RIDOH website here:
>
> http:health.ri.gov/lists/disciplinaryactions/.

The referenced website for Rochelle Fortin said, "No Disciplinary Actions."

On February 3, 2022, Attorney Devereaux responded to Ms. Mello via email:

> Ms. Mello: Bill Devereaux here. Am I to understand that the Board has closed the investigation? My client, who is copied on this email, is concerned that he has not had an investigator from the RIDOH speak to him or attempt to contact him. He believes that it is very material for an investigator and the Board to understand how this unethical treatment has affected him.

You also have my permission to copy Ted Blickwedel on any communications and/or to speak with him directly.

Bill Devereaux

Devereaux did not receive response or communications from Ms. Mello or anyone else at the RIDOH.

On March 9, 2022, Attorney Devereaux wrote a letter to Ms. Mello. The following are excerpts from that correspondence:

> On February 2nd, 2022, nine days after the January 24th letter, I received correspondence from you regarding Mr. Blickwedel's complaint. In that letter, you advise that RIDOH had now completed a "thorough review" of the complaint which included "a review of all material provided by you, communications with parties involved, and a comprehension of applicable Rhode Island law." I also forwarded this document to my client.
>
> I must advise you that Mr. Blickwedel was dismayed, and I was disappointed, to learn neither he nor his witnesses were ever contacted by representatives of the Board as inferred in your February 2nd correspondence. After being initially advised that a thorough investigation would likely take some time, it could not be ignored that apparently this investigation took less that nine days.

In an interview with Ted, he expressed concerns that the RIDOH had perhaps not thoroughly investigated his claim as they did not want to be involved in something that might tarnish the Veterans Administration and particularly the Vet Center Program.

Attorney Devereaux's letter to Ms. Mello addressed this concern in his letter:

> Blickwedel is justifiably concerned that his complaint has not and will not receive proper consideration and that the board simply does not want to get involved in the matter. He understood that the subject of this complaint worked within the VA system and that the VA mental health care system, itself, could potentially come under scrutiny. He was therefore worried that the Board would shy away from thoroughly investigating his complaint for this and other related reasons, even though the Board is obligated to do so according to the RIDOH code of regulations, Title 216, Chapter 40.

Several items stand out from the correspondence:

1   The RIDOH volunteered that the investigation would take a long period of time. In fact, the investigation took nine days.

2   Ms. Mello claimed that the claimant, Ted Blickwedel, and the four witnesses had been contacted. That was not true, as none of the five had heard from anyone.

3   And as further outlined in Devereaux's letter, "The complaint clearly demonstrated violations of ethical behavior, in accordance with the NASW Code of Ethics. However, the Board still chose not to investigate these allegations, which is contrary to the RIDOH Regulations since they incorporate the NASW Code of Ethics into these statues."

Were the RIDOH actions or lack of action a cover-up? If so, why would they choose to abrogate their responsibilities and not conduct a thorough investigation? Are they protecting someone? Who? Why?

Why would the RIDOH, through its inaction, condone unethical behavior, that in part led to ongoing compromised Veteran's mental health care?

Did Rochelle Fortin act alone?

Where was management, Mike Fisher? Has Mike Fisher investigated or taken any action regarding Fortin's alleged ethics violations? If not, why not? Did Fortin act alone? Was she directed by management or have their approval to take these actions?

Why did he not pursue Fortin's ethical violations which he is obligated to do under the NASW Code of Ethics, after having received a copy of the letter sent to Fortin by Devereaux regarding the false statements made when filing for the No Trespass order?

The people of Rhode Island, all U.S. citizens, Veterans, VA VET Center counselors, and Ted Blickwedel have been ill-served.

The Rhode Island Department of Health slammed the door on the face of accepted ethical behaviors.

Turning a blind eye on unethical behavior by the RIDOH is outrageous.

So, here is the real issue: Is there anyone else in Rhode Island, anyone on the state or federal level who has the courage to speak truth to power? Who will join Ted in his crusade for the ethical treatment of Veterans and counselors?

Will you?

CHAPTER 10

Post Traumatic Stress Disorder

Throughout history, dating as far back as Homer's *The Iliad*, Shakespeare's *Henry IV*, and Charles Dicken's *A Tale of Two Cities*, symptoms following traumatic experiences describe what modern medicine now defines as Post Traumatic Stress Disorder (PTSD).

Different types of traumas can precipitate the onset of PTSD, including war-zone trauma, assault, rape, torture, childhood physical and sexual abuse, natural and technological disasters, serious accidents, and chronic diseases.

In the 18th century, these symptoms were referred to as *nostalgia* when addressing PTSD symptoms displaying by soldiers. This referred to exhibiting homesickness, depression, anxiety, and sleep disorders.

Another health-related issue was called *Soldier's heart*, which indicated cardiac issues and problems breathing.

In WWII, Combat Stress Reaction and *battle fatigue* were used interchangeably to describe many of the symptoms that is now referred to as PTSD.

It was not until 1952 that the American Psychiatric Association (APA) included *Gross Stress Reaction* in their catalog of mental disorders, an anxiety disorder. The study of Gross Stress Reaction over the last seven decades has led to many revisions as to its causes, treatments, and prognoses.

Every year, more than 8 million people in the United States struggle with Post Traumatic Stress Disorder (PTSD) along with another 350 million people worldwide. PTSD can create intense physical, emotional, and mental distress, and if left untreated, it can lead to long-term psychological and physiological damage.

Approximately 50 percent of the population in the United States report exposure to traumatic events. PTSD prevalence rates are around 10–12 percent for women and 5–6 percent for men, with about an overall 7 percent lifetime prevalence rate for PTSD (Carr, 2004; Lee & Young, 2001; Ozer & Weiss, 2004; Schnurr, Friedman & Bernardy, 2002).

It is not only more prevalent in women, but according to some studies conducted with Vietnam veterans (Friedman, 2004; James & Gilliand, 2005), it was estimated that 30 percent of males and 26 percent of females in this population had PTSD from their military service.

The VA VET Center program, established by federal legislation in 1979, was created in direct response to veterans not receiving the personal mental health care for a myriad of issues, primarily treatment of PTSD and associated illnesses.

The following is taken from the US Department of Veterans Affairs website:

PTSD is no longer an anxiety disorder. PTSD is sometimes associated with other mood states (for example, depression) and with angry or reckless behavior rather than anxiety. So, PTSD is now in a new category, Trauma and Stressor-Related Disorders. PTSD includes four different types of symptoms:

1 Reliving the traumatic event, also called re-experiencing or intrusion (i.e., nightmares, visual flashbacks, intrusive thoughts and triggered cues to reminders of the event).

2 Avoiding situations that are reminders of the event (i.e., avoidance of thoughts and behaviors related to the event; avoidance of activities, places or people reminiscent of the trauma; psychogenic amnesia; diminished interest in significant activities; emotional numbing and detachment from others).

3 Negative changes in beliefs and feelings (e.g., about self and/or the world).

4 Feeling keyed up, also called hyperarousal or over-reactive to situations (i.e., irritability and anger outbursts, difficulty falling and staying asleep, concentration problems, hypervigilance and startle responses).

Most people experience some of these symptoms after a traumatic event, so PTSD is not diagnosed unless all four types of symptoms last for at least a month and cause significant distress or problems with day-to-day functioning. Also, these symptoms must have been brought on by exposure to an event in which the person experienced, witnessed, or was confronted with actual or threatened death or serious injury, or threat to physical integrity of self or others and in which the person's response involved intense fear, helplessness and/or horror.

Although some form of post-combat disorder has affected many combatants in every war, investigation of the long-term effects of combat exposure did not occur until after the Vietnam conflict (Herman, 1997). With the return of veterans from the Vietnam conflict (1964-1973), some veterans established peer support (rap) groups and coined the term Post-Vietnam Syndrome. Post-Vietnam Syndrome included intrusive thoughts and nightmares related to combat, numbed responsiveness, and other manifestations such as substance dependence, depression, anxiety and rage (Friedman, 1981).

The following description reflects the overwhelming reality so many men and women have experienced and continue to experience. Those having witnessed these characteristics in others will immediately take note.

PTSD is often accompanied by comorbid medical and psychiatric disorders, especially alcohol or substance abuse, depression and/or anxiety (Zatzick et al, 1997; Friedman, 2005a). Biopsychological changes affect cognitive processing, memory and coping abilities, which contribute to impaired interpersonal relations in marital, family, social and employment settings.

Further, their research indicated that veterans with PTSD also had physical limitations, impaired role function, compromised physical health and decreased well-being (Zatzick et al., 1997). The lack of public support for Vietnam Veterans likely complicated readjustment to civilian life and exacerbated some cases of PTSD (Friedman, 2005a).

Litz (2007) reported that Vietnam veterans who used social supports to disclose personal problems or deployment experiences were less likely to have PTSD per Green et al. (1990), whereas lack of family cohesion predicted the development of PTSD in Gulf veterans per Sutker et al. (1995).

When conducting interviews with veterans during the course of researching this book, the most often referenced post-combat trauma is outlined below:

Stress and adversity after deployment also affect the degree of post-traumatic impairments (Litz, 2007). The homecoming experience significantly affects a veteran's readjustment to civilian life (Friedman, 2005a). The war must not be confused with the warrior (Friedman, 2004). As with all veterans, a combat veteran's adaptation and readjustment to civilian life must be supported with consideration of individual variables in an ecological context.

Earlier in the book, it was pointed out that every client is unique. PTSD affects each person differently. This is the crux of the problem as it relates to the clinical productivity policy change that is being arbitrarily forced on VET Center clients and counselors by VA RCS management. In many instances, this has resulted in clinicians not having enough time to implement the best treatment approach which best fits the individual's needs and circumstances, since they are expected to achieve the required visit count which does not permit this. This is also especially true since counselors have reported they continue to be given additional administrative duties, even after Ted Blickwedel initially addressed these issues with VET Center Program officials in January 2018.

The following conclusion points directly to the need for personal and individual treatment for veteran clients:

> *Veterans suffering from PTSD and associated mental health issues require personal individualized treatment demanding flexibility in the therapy and services being offered.* We are not "numbers," but human beings desperate for professional care that meet our needs, not "production requirements" mandated by ill-advised bureaucrats.

Treatment

For almost four decades there have been a variety of interventions used to treat PTSD. The most prevalent treatment approaches have often involved Cognitive Behavior Therapy (CBT), Eye Movement Desensitization & Reprocessing (EMDR), Prolonged Exposure (PE) and Cognitive Processing Therapy (CPT). All of these strategies have been validated by research studies to be effective evidenced-based treatments that help alleviate PTSD symptoms.

The evidence suggests that CBT has a greater impact than specific kinds of drug therapy in the treatment of PTSD, but EMDR demonstrated that it might be significantly more effective than CBT. Further, the outcome of EMDR treatment in a few instances also indicated that it may have a greater rapidity of effect compared to other treatment approaches, and for a longer duration. The significant results associated with EMDR as an efficacious PTSD treatment intervention is additionally supported by other multiple controlled studies (as cited in Shapiro, 2002).

However, there are numerous studies which also suggest the weight of evidence supports the use of CBT for treating PTSD over EMDR. Research of EMDR indicates it is beneficial, but the quality of EMDR studies and the delineation of active mechanisms are not as strong to date as those for CBT (as cited in Hamblen et al., 2006).

The dominant treatment interventions for PTSD with combat veterans have been PE, EMDR, and other cognitive-behavioral coping skills (Emmelkamp, 1994; Foa & Meadows, 1997; Rothbaum et al., 2000; Van Etten & Taylor, 1998). For many traumatized clients, including combat veterans, results are generally positive for reducing physiological arousal, intrusive traumatic thoughts, sleep disturbance, fear and anxiety.

Although treatment outcomes for combat veterans with PTSD have been somewhat encouraging, research findings conclude that no one of these traditional therapeutic interventions alone can successfully relieve the myriad of intrusive and incapacitating symptoms that accompany the condition for long periods of time (Seidler & Wagner, 2006).

Further, a study published in the *Journal of Traumatic Stress* found that nine in every ten of the 49,425 veterans of the Iraq and Afghan wars who sought care from VA facilities for newly diagnosed PTSD dropped out before completing treatment as recommended.

A comprehensive study published in the Journal of the American Medical Association (JAMA) found that approximately two-thirds of service members and veterans completing a course of Prolonged Exposure or Cognitive Processing Therapy, in peer-reviewed studies published between 1980 and 2015, still met PTSD diagnostic criteria after treatment.

Additionally, more research is necessary that directly focuses on combat veterans with PTSD because of the impact on them, their families and communities, society at large; and particularly because the effects of this disorder are passed on from generation to generation.

For over 20 years energy psychology methods have evolved to treat PTSD, trauma and other psychosocial issues. These strategies are more focused, goal oriented and active than conventional therapies. They work with the body's energy systems (e.g., meridians, chakras) to create a change in one's perception and experience.

Most non-energy psychotherapies engage only thought and emotion. However, energy psychology activates emotion, cognition, the physical body and energy system within a single session. This may be why energy psychology approaches appear to work more quickly than conventional psychotherapy.

The Association for Comprehensive Energy Psychology (ACEP) is a charitable nonprofit, professional organization dedicated to the research, education and promotion of energy psychology and energy practices among health professionals and the public throughout the world. Their goal is to resolve the effects of stress and trauma and optimize well-being by integrating energy psychology and energy practices throughout community and healthcare systems.

While ACEP endorses a variety of efficacious energy psychology interventions, they predominantly focus on Emotional Freedom Techniques (EFT) and Thought Field Therapy.

On their website (*www.energypsych.org*), ACEP summarizes the research and provides a comprehensive list of studies that document the effectiveness of energy psychology methods. This is what they have reported to date on their website:

- In total, 275+ review articles, research studies and meta-analyses have been published in professional, peer-reviewed journals.

- 125+ Studies Document Energy Psychology's effectiveness (70+ randomized controlled trials & 55+ clinical outcome studies).

- 5 meta-analyses show effective treatment for depression, anxiety and PTSD.

- 8 studies comparing cognitive behavior therapy (CBT) and energy psychology (EP) show that EP is either equivalent to or more effective than CBT. And in several studies, EP achieved results in significantly less time.

- In comparison with Exposure Therapy for the treatment of PTSD, EFT was significantly more effective in reducing hyperarousal, anxiety, and depression symptoms, with reductions following the EFT treatments remaining consistent at 12-month follow-up.

- When compared to Eye Movement Desensitization and Reprocessing (EMDR) in the treatment of PTSD, both EMDR and EFT were effective within a mean of less than four sessions.

- Studies show 86 percent of 49 war veterans no longer had PTSD symptoms after 6 hour-long EFT sessions. It's 2 times as effective and 2 times faster than prolonged exposure therapy. This has been replicated with similar outcomes (Church et al, 2013; Church, Sparks & Clond, 2016; Church et al, 2016).

Overall, it appears that EFT is proving to be more successful than other therapies when it comes to treating PTSD. It also has the following advantages:

- Fewer treatment sessions are required.
- Treatment effects typically show significant reductions in symptoms and their impact, and these improvements tend to be longer lasting.
- Low risk of negative side effects, even when treating highly traumatized individuals.
- Minimum training needed since a seasoned clinician can learn and begin applying a basic protocol very quickly.
- Unlike many psychotherapy methods that require one-on-one sessions, EFT can be highly effective when delivered to groups. This makes it suitable for combat battalions returning from deployment, refugees living in camps, caregivers returning from humanitarian missions, and children in classrooms.

For millions of people with PTSD, energy psychology, specifically EFT, offers much-needed hope and relief. It is a powerful intervention that continues to be confirmed as an effective antidote to living with the pain of PTSD.

In July 2010, David Feinstein and Dawson Church who are two renowned practitioners and researchers of energy psychology and EFT, testified before the House Veterans Affairs Committee's hearing on "Innovative Treatments for PTSD." They testified how EFT is an effective intervention to successfully treat veterans with PTSD, based on several studies conducted by doctors through the Iraq Vets Stress Project (www.stressproject.org). Earlier this same month, three members of Congress sent a letter to the VA Secretary at the time, Eric Shinseki, requesting that he inform VA clinicians about the effectiveness of EFT.

On September 20, 2013, Ohio Congressman Tim Ryan sent a follow-up letter to Secretary Shinseki urging him to designate EFT as an approved evidence-based therapy in the VA, since EFT had been established by the American Psychological Association (APA) to be an *empirically validated treatment* for PTSD.

In 2017, the VA added EFT to List 2, approving it as a *generally safe therapy*. However, it has not yet been added to List 1 as an approved treatment. This is in spite of the fact EFT continues to demonstrate quick results to alleviate PTSD symptoms in veterans, with longer lasting results compared to other conventional evidenced-based interventions.

Why has the VA not endorsed EFT as a valid best practices approach to treat veterans with PTSD when research has overwhelmingly supported its efficacy? How much longer are veterans going to be denied this treatment strategy which is in their best interest? Who is going to ensure veterans have access to EFT treatment within the VA medical centers and VET Center program?

CHAPTER 11

Whistleblowers of America (WoA)

Ted Blickwedel turned to Whistleblowers of America following his retirement from the VET Center. The organization was founded to assist whistleblowers who have suffered retaliation after having identified harm to individuals or the public.

After having utilized the WoA resources, Ted made it his mission to support the efforts of the organization and those who have been or are considering becoming whistleblowers. His interest in WoA is a result of the experiences he encountered as a whistleblower. It is his goal to assist in educating and empowering whistleblowers.

What is Whistleblowing

(Resourced from the WoA website: *www.whistleblowersofamerica.org*)

Whistleblowers are everywhere and can be any employee (including military personnel) who sees wrongdoing and speaks out to stop it. However, it is often a lonely and confusing legal process. In the news media, we hear stories of victims who have waited decades before coming forward or have had to work for years to gather enough evidence to be credible. Yet, they protect individuals and the public from all kinds of harm, ranging from medical errors to toxic contamination to financial fraud to discrimination and sexual abuse. Whistleblowers are the first relators of wrongdoing.

Whistleblowers are essential parts of the workplace, and the main reason injustice is brought to light. When someone takes a stand and reports evidence about the corrupt actions employers and supervisors perpetrate for personal gain, it evens the playing field and dispels the inequality between the workers and employers.

Unfortunately, many in the position who blow the whistle face workplace abuse and loss of job opportunities. People believe those who *snitch* on their superiors don't deserve protection. In some societies, whistleblowers are equated with traitors and liars. Without them, employers could freely embezzle, harass their employees, and destroy the lives of the public without consequence.

The WoA was founded by a one-time whistleblower, Jacqueline Garrick. Ms. Garrick, a graduate of Temple University, majored in social work. She spent time as an intern at the VA Medical Center in Coatesville, PA and then became the program director for the Vietnam Veterans Resource Center in New York. Her time at the VA found her involved with treating veterans for PTSD. In 1992 she joined the US Army as a social work officer. After separating from the army, she became the American Legion's Deputy Director of Healthcare. Years later she was appointed by the Obama administration to the Department of Defense's Undersecretary of Defense for Personnel and Readiness Office.

In 2014, Ms. Garrick found herself in a position where she was retaliated against for exposing conflict of interest and alleged fraud in government contract awards. In other words, she found herself adrift and casting about for ways to resolve her professional dilemma, while at the same time moving forward with her original concerns centered around the subject of her whistleblowing.

Separated from her employment, Ms. Garrick decided to take what she had learned from her whistleblowing experience and utilize her administrative and social worker skills helping other whistleblowers. In 2017, Ms. Garrick founded Whistleblowers of America.

Ms. Garrick's persistence paid off when she was recognized by The Government Accountability Project:

> Government Accountability Project congratulates Jacqueline Garrick, founder of Whistleblowers of America (WoA), on her recent victory at the MSPB following a years-long battle after blowing the whistle on attempted contracting fraud and tragic mission breakdowns at the Department of Defense's Defense Suicide Prevention Office (DSPO).

In a May 11, 2020, decision, Administrative Judge Andrew M. Dunnaville held that according to a stipulation, Garrick was subjected to "retaliation and hostile work environment," and that based on a preponderance of evidence, she was entitled to retirement benefits that had been denied to her for over three years. Unfortunately, it is too often the case that government truth-tellers do not enjoy this victorious result and instead suffer through the exhausting, if not debilitating process of blowing the whistle. It takes true strength of character and determination to undergo the rigors of this process.

WoA helps those who have suffered retaliation from whistleblowing. WoA provides peer mentoring support, education, training, and is engaged in public advocacy campaigns on behalf of whistleblowers.

Ms. Garrick has testified before Congress on many occasions regarding whistleblowing. She speaks to whistleblower protection, the role whistleblowers have in society, rampant sexual assault in the military, its impact on male and female veterans and other topics relating to whistleblowers.

She is a perennial advocate for veterans and PTSD awareness.

Ms. Garrick has authored the *Whistleblowers of America Peer Support Mentor Training Manual: Peer Support in Overcoming the Toxic Tactics of Whistleblower Retaliation.* Part of the description for her book reads:

> Whistleblowers of America Peer Support Mentor Training Manual is designed to assist whistleblowers overcome the toxic tactics of retaliation and discover their resilience through a peer-to-peer connection. Ms. Garrick has created a Whistleblower Retaliation Checklist© and describes the elements of retaliation as gaslighting, mobbing, marginalizing, shunning, devaluing, blackballing, double-binding, accusing and physical and emotional violence.

The Whistleblower Retaliation Checklist and further information on the toxic relation tactics typically used by bureaucracies to silence those who report organizational misconduct can be found in the September 2020 article she wrote which was published in an international journal, *Crisis, Stress, and Human Resilience,* entitled "Whistleblower Retaliation Checklist: A New Instrument for Identifying Retaliatory Tactics and Their Psychosocial Impacts after an Employee Discloses Workplace Wrongdoing." It can be accessed at the following link: *https:// www.crisisjournal.org/article/17219-whistleblower-retaliation-checklist-a-new-instrument-for-identifying-retaliatory-tactics-and-their-psychosocial-impacts-after-an-employee-discloses-workplace-wrongdoing.*

Ms. Garrick, in an article published in the Smithfield, RI magazine, *The Valley Breeze,* commented on Ted's involvement with WoA:

> "Blickwedel's research and questioning will bring change to the VA that could save thousands of lives, as well as create job opportunities across the country." She said the WoA also helps people such as Blickwedel bring about change in Congress. "We're trying to hold the VA accountable for the retaliation they inflicted on him."

Ted has served on various WoA-sponsored panels and discussion groups to further the work of WoA. On July 30, 2021, he was part of a WoA panel celebrating National Whistleblowers Day. During the discussion, he was queried about mental, emotional and spiritual healing techniques he employed to cope with the trauma he experienced.

This is what Ted shared:

> I used a combination of proven strategies that were therapeutically beneficial to process and alleviate the traumatic impact from the retaliation I was experiencing. Not only did these interventions significantly relieve my anxiety and depression, but they also helped keep me grounded and constructively focused. This really allowed me to develop and maintain much needed resilience to successfully function and cope with the stress I was subjected to. *Eventually, I was able to completely stop taking psychiatric medication.*

The specific methods Ted used are outlined below.

- Energy Psychology Interventions, such as Emotional Freedom Techniques (EFT), which are effective evidenced-based trauma treatment strategies that are promoted by the Association for Comprehensive Energy Psychology (ACEP – *www.energypsych.org*).
- Wisdom Healing Chi Gong (QiGong) with Master Mingtong Gu (www.chicenter.com).
- Meditation and other Mindfulness Techniques.
- Therapeutic and Deep Tissue Massage Therapy.
- A Week-long Therapeutic Intensive in July 2018 involving Shamanic Healing Techniques, EFT, Dream Work, and Family Constellations (*Health, Happiness, & Family Constellations* by Michael Reddy).
- Healthy Lifestyle, to include a nutritious diet and regular exercise.

Ted went on to explain what he did following his early retirement, in his determined pursuit to *speak truth to power* and hold VET Center management accountable and right the wrong they had perpetuated.

He also spoke to the importance of media in the whistleblower process. "If you do not have the media engaged in your story, in all likelihood you will be ignored, and your cause will fail." His application of the adherence to this principle is outlined in Chapter 16, The VET Center Improvement Act.

There is Strength in Numbers is a blog that Ted contributed to in recognition of National Whistleblower Day. In the blog, Ted outlines items whistleblowers should consider in their high stakes endeavor. The following highlights content from the blog:

> I am a retired Marine who is a combat and disabled veteran. From January 2009 until February 2018, I conducted individual and group therapy with combat veterans at the Warwick, RI Veteran's Center for the Readjustment Counseling Service (RCS), a branch of the Veterans Health Administration (VHA).
>
> I officially retired in April 2018, three years earlier than I had intended, due to the oppressive and unethical clinical *productivity expectations* instituted by RCS in 2016 that negatively affected the health and well-being of counselors and degraded our ability to provide quality care to veterans. RCS

leadership failed to acknowledge and address these issues when it was brought to their attention numerous times through the normal chain of command, including *emails sent on January 18 and 25, 2018.* Subsequently, I filed grievances with various federal agencies (e.g., VA OIG, OSC, and ORM/EEO) to report these excessive and unreasonable mandates, as well as the retaliation I experienced from RCS/VET Center Program management after raising my concerns.

There are several factors I learned that were essential to the success of my advocacy efforts and are crucial to a favorable outcome for any whistleblower campaign. For those who are compelled to undertake similar crusades, these indispensable guidelines are outlined below so they can enhance their chances for an effective effort and positive result.

1 **Instances of misconduct and its consequences** that are being reported, to include retaliation and its impact, **need to be well-documented** through written material, recordings, witnesses, and/or relevant research that validates the allegations. This kind of evidence is important to establish credibility.

2 **Solicit support from as many colleagues and peers as possible** to back your advocacy campaign since there is strength in numbers when you are on a united front, both for the cause and your emotional sustenance. However, realize that most coworkers and associates will be afraid to stand with you because they fear reprisals. This is typically due to reacting out of survival instincts to protect themselves, so don't take it personally.

3 **Enlist assistance from family, friends, reputable whistleblowing organizations** to serve as confidants and

sources of encouragement, especially during difficult times in the process, to help maintain a healthy and balanced mental state. I highly recommend the *National Whistleblower Center* and *Whistleblowers of America* since they are knowledgeable and experienced with whistleblowing and its ramifications. This is important prior to forging ahead with your initiative, in order to be prepared and help minimize the adverse impact that can evolve from whistleblower retaliation, as well as develop a better understanding of available resources and effective strategies.

4   **Obtaining media coverage to raise awareness** and gain the backing of politicians and/or other influential entities is crucial so the successful achievement of your objectives will be greatly enhanced and produce authentic change that is truly beneficial. This will also potentially foster significant momentum which can be motivating and inspiring to keep pushing forward.

5   **Stay connected with your support network** and keep them updated to maintain their interest and involvement. Sustaining these relationships with colleagues, family, friends, centers of influence, and organizations is imperative to retain their backing by participating in spreading the word and promoting appropriate action regarding your campaign through emails, social media, and contacting their Congressional Delegates to endorse your efforts.

6   **Exhibit a professional, tactful, and composed demeanor throughout all your interactions** with media contacts, politicians, other supporters, and adversaries. It is vital, too, to be organized, clear, and succinct with what you say and how you articulate your message. This will help facilitate greater receptiveness to what you are communicating.

Whistleblowers of America is funded by Ms. Garrick and through donations from concerned individuals like you. Information on learning more and donating to WoA can be obtained on their website: *www.whistleblowersofamerica.org.*

CHAPTER 12

Congress Mandated GAO Investigation

Ted Blickwedel contacted Senator Reed (D-RI) and Congressman Cicilline (D-RI) regarding the VET Center management's handling of the productivity mandate and the subsequent retaliation he experienced.

Senators Reed and Tester (D-MT) requested the Government Accountability Office (GAO) investigate.

The following is a summary of the GAO findings:

Summary of GAO Report on VA VET Center Productivity Expectations

The GAO concluded in their report from the investigation they conducted that VET Center productivity expectations could negatively affect client care and create undue burden and stress on counselors providing that care. They also revealed that the VA has not evaluated how these expectations may affect veteran care or counselor practices, and that such evaluations would be consistent with federal standards for internal control. They conveyed that without a systematic evaluation and periodic reassessment of VET Center counselor productivity expectations, the VA/RCS does not have a good understanding how the effects of these expectations could adversely impact counselors' practices and potentially client care. Consequently, the GAO recommended that VA/RCS management should establish and operate reoccurring monitoring activities, evaluate the results, and remediate any deficiencies in a timely manner, so that there is reasonable assurance that the productivity expectations are working as intended and do not have any unintended or negative effects on counselor practices and veteran care.

Additionally, the GAO found that the VET Center Program does not have an effective systematic way for reporting concerns about the effects of the productivity expectations up reporting lines beyond VET Center Directors, and they indicated this is essential to help ensure officials are responsive to the needs of their staff, as well as to the needs of veterans and their families. They further stated it is important that an evaluation of the productivity expectations include obtaining systematic feedback from counselors on any Recommendations for Executive Action on client care.

It was also noted by the GAO that the VET Center program does not have an adequate staffing model to accurately identify staffing needs, since their existing method does not fully adhere to key practices, as documented in their report. They determined, because of this, that the VA/RCS is at risk of making decisions about VET Center staffing requirements that may be misinformed and not responsive to changing veterans' needs, especially with the increasing veteran demand for mental health services in the VA/VET Center Program. Therefore, due to the critical importance of ensuring appropriate VET

Center staffing, the GAO additionally recommended that VA/RCS management develops and implements a VET Center staffing model which incorporates key practices in the design of staffing models, and that these models be updated regularly with time frames for assessment, and to employ any needed changes as warranted.

The GAO further stipulated in their commentary that they are sending copies of the report to appropriate congressional committees, the Secretary of Veterans Affairs, and other interested parties. They also specified that they would provide updated information when they confirm what actions have been taken by the VA/VET Center Program in response to their recommendations.

Ted Blickwedel prepared an analysis of the GAO findings and presented it to Senator Reed and Congressman Cicilline.

The analysis emphasized the need to protect counselors from retaliation for offering their opinions on current policies. It also emphasized that the VA/VET Center management must provide an independent monitoring system for counselors to make their concerns known to management.

The analysis makes mention of the VA response to the report stating "RCS officials told them that later this fiscal year they plan to change how the visits expectation is calculated to simplify the communication about it, *but it will not be substantially different from the current version.*" These officials also told the GAO that they do not have plans to make other updates at this time but believe their plan to annually review performance standards for all counselors—which includes the productivity expectations—*would be sufficient for periodic reassessment.*

Ted's analysis goes on to highlight that the VA/VET Center management had no intention of adopting any of the GAO recommendations.

The report concludes policies and guidelines must be established in the VA/VET Center Program designed to address GAO recommendations and protect clients and counselors from an unaccountable RCS management.

GAO VET CENTER REPORT

(GAO-20-652)
September 30, 2020
Concerns About VA Response

Issues

The Government Accountability Office (GAO) conducted an investigation into the negative impact productivity expectations might be having on quality care and counselor welfare within the Veteran Administration (VA)/VET Center Program. The GAO released their report on September 23, 2020; and concluded that VET Center productivity expectations could adversely affect client care and create undue burden and stress on counselors providing that care. They also revealed that the VA has not evaluated how these expectations may affect veteran care or counselor practices, and that such evaluations would be consistent with federal standards for internal control. They conveyed that without a systematic evaluation and periodic reassessment of VET Center counselor productivity expectations, the VA/RCS does not have a good understanding how the effects of these expectations could negatively impact counselors' practices and potentially clients' care. Consequently, the GAO recommended that VA/RCS management should establish and operate reoccurring monitoring activities, evaluate the results, and remediate any deficiencies in a timely manner, *so that there is reasonable assurance that the productivity expectations are working as intended and do not have any unintended or negative effects on counselor practices and veteran care.*

Veterans Administration officials told the GAO, in response to the GAO findings, they do not have plans to make other updates at this time but "believe their plan to annually review performance standards for all counselors—which includes the productivity expectations—*would be sufficient for periodic reassessment.*"

This reply by VA/RCS management is grossly inadequate to rectify the adverse impact of excessive productivity expectations on quality care and counselor well-being. Saying they plan to change how they calculate the visits expectation, but that it won't be substantially different from the current version, is basically conveying they intend to do what they have been doing all along. These are the same responses they have been telling counselors over the last four years when these issues have been brought to their attention. Some counselors have experienced retaliation when trying to draw attention to this. Subsequently, as substantiated in documents which have been provided to the GAO via Senator Reed (D-RI), *many counselors have given up and are afraid to speak up due to fear of reprisals.* Only simplifying the communication about how the visits expectation is calculated, *without reducing it to an acceptable level,* is not going to adequately resolve the problem that unreasonable production standards are having by diminishing counselor welfare and degrading their ability to provide quality care. This is supported by numerous other counselors in the VET Center Program who were *not* afraid to come forward regarding these concerns, many of whom were not interviewed during this inquiry when the GAO was requested to do so. Furthermore, The RCS *Clinical Capacity Report,* which was forwarded to the GAO by Senator Reed's staff, fundamentally came to the same conclusion. Therefore, the existing plan of RCS to annually review the performance standards for counselors, including productivity expectations, is *not* sufficient to ascertain the actual extent to which the visit count standards are negatively affecting client care and counselor well-being when this only serves to see if counselors are achieving the production metrics themselves.

Additionally, the GAO found that the VET Center program does not have an effective systematic way for reporting concerns about the effects of the productivity expectations up reporting lines beyond VET Center directors, and they indicated this is essential to help ensure officials are responsive to the needs of their staff, as well as to the needs of veterans and their families. They further stated in their report that it is important for an evaluation of the productivity expectations to include obtaining systematic feedback from counselors on any Recommendations for Executive Action on client care. Subsequently, the GAO also recommended that VA/RCS management must acquire ongoing systematic input from counselors on any potentially negative effects on client care.

On page 31 of the GAO Report, VA/RCS management, in response to the GAO's recommendation regarding "obtaining systematic feedback from counselors on any potential negative effects on client care," mentioned that systematic feedback from counselors will include direct information on both the positive and potentially negative effects on client care and training needs, appropriate data provided which is received through customer feedback, available productivity and capacity data, and existing surveying to include the annual All Employee Survey and what is reported by counselors during site visits.

Again, this answer by VA officials is completely lacking in credibility since these are already the methods by which they attain feedback from counselors, which has proven to be ineffective so far. An example of this is in the report where the GAO cites on page 14, "that the VA's annual All Employees' Survey was not a satisfactory feedback channel because there is not enough space to explain what is occurring with regards to the productivity expectations." Once more, VA/RCS leadership is pronouncing they are going to do the same thing going forward in the way they currently collect information from counselors. This is unacceptable since counselor's voices will continue to not be heard, unless there is a mechanism that will allow for effective feedback in a manner which is centralized, not suppressed, and that cannot be ignored. If this does not change, then counselors' suggestions and concerns will never be incorporated into managements' decisions so they will decrease production expectations, when necessary, in order to avoid negative impacts on counselor health and welfare, as well as the adverse effect this would have on delivery of quality care to veterans and their families.

Recommendations

1   A separate anonymous online bilateral survey should be developed by a team of RCS Counselors and VET Center directors, in conjunction with the GAO or a third party outside of the VA, that adequately addresses any negative impact which productivity expectations are having on client care and counselor health, welfare, and practices. Also, the GAO, the designated third party outside of the VA, and members of Congress should be able to directly access the results of this survey independently from VA/RCS management, where no parties can alter the content of the survey. This would ensure that feedback from counselors is not edited, suppressed, and/or dismissed by RCS officials, which would permit the GAO, the designated third party outside of the VA, and members of appropriate Congressional Committees to accurately view the content of the survey first hand. Consequently, the GAO and Congressional Oversight Committees would have more precise and truthful information which they could use to make sure that VA/RCS management is truly being held accountable to

implement any necessary adjustments when needed so that visit count metrics and other production standards do not have an adverse effect on quality care and counselor well-being within the VET Center program.

2   Because of the concerns that were addressed, and to ensure full intended compliance with the GAO recommendations, it is suggested that the first two recommendations on pages 23 and 31 of the report be amended to clearly specify actions the RCS Chief Officer must take to make certain that productivity expectations do not have a negative impact on client care and counselor welfare, as follows:

   a   **Recommendation 1:** The Undersecretary for Health should ensure the RCS Chief Officer evaluates VET Center productivity expectations for counselors, including (1) obtaining systematic and unaltered feedback from counselors, through new methods that are objective and effective, on any potentially negative effects on client care and counselor practices/well-being; and (2) determining whether directors and counselors need additional training or guidance on how the expectations are calculated.

   b   **Recommendation 2:** The Undersecretary for Health should ensure the RCS Chief Officer develops a plan and time frames for periodically reassessing its productivity expectations for counselors and implementing any needed changes as appropriate to mitigate whatever adverse effect productivity expectations are having on veteran care and counselor well-being.

3   There should be a collaborative effort between the GAO, House and Senate Committees on Veterans Affairs, and the VA/RCS to make sure all these concerns are sufficiently addressed, to include incorporating these recommendations into VA/RCS policy and operations so that productivity expectations genuinely do not have any negative impact on quality care and counselor welfare.

CHAPTER 13

RCS Grievance Summary

The following is a verbatim copy of a report compiled by Ted Blickwedel. It outlines the Issues, provides background, reveals the impact on the VET Center's clients and counselors, details the sequence of events, illuminates what research shows, draws conclusions, and makes recommendations.

Readjustment Counseling Service (RCS) Grievance Summary

Issues

- Quantitative clinical visit count mandate having a negative impact on the health and well-being of counselors, which has degraded their ability to provide quality care to veterans.

- Personnel reprisals against me and other clinicians who speak up about these concerns.

Background

- RCS is part of the Veterans Health Administration (VHA) and provides clinical services to combat veterans and their families.

- Counselors were required to spend 40 percent of their time on direct service and 50 percent of their time on overall clinical functions.

- Around 2012-2013 these percentages changed to 50 percent and 60 percent respectively, which was still fair and manageable.

- March 1, 2016: The RCS Acting Chief Officer (Charles Flora) instituted another quantitative clinical measure that was added to the expected production standard, which mandated the number of visits a counselor was supposed to have. It is computed by multiplying hours worked per week by 1.5 and dividing this by 2, which results in the total expected visits per week a counselor should have ($40 \times 1.5 / 2 = 30$). This figure is then divided into the number of actual visits that gives you a percentage which is the proportion of actual visits to total expected visits (example: 25.5 actual visits / 30 expected visits = 85%). The overall visit count expressed as this percentage is expected to be 85% or over. This basically equates to counselors being required to spend at least 75% of their time in session with veterans and/or their family members, if a counselor has 30 individual/family visits that each last 50–60 minutes which is the normal industry length of time for a session. However, conducting group sessions can reduce this percentage of direct service time, but there are a multitude of counselors who have caseloads that are not always clinically appropriate for group counseling.

- This visit count expectation is too difficult to accomplish in conjunction with other required administrative duties, since it does not allow enough time to perform these other functions (i.e., progress notes, treatment plans, assessments, release-of-information correspondence, record audits, case closings, outreach events, etc.).

- These performance standards do not account for more time that is needed with complex cases, crisis intervention, and family and couples' sessions. They also do not allow enough time to conduct trauma treatment with the combat veterans who suffer from PTSD, which sometimes requires more than 60 minutes per session to do this properly with evidenced-based interventions.

- Clinicians, too, do not have any control over clients who cancel or do not show for an appointment, or the number of new referrals that come to their VET Center, and therefore, should not be held responsible for this.

- Counselors who do not meet this clinical visit count expectation have been threatened with negative consequences (e.g., made aware of deficiency in writing, complete a Performance Improvement Plan (PIP) with deadlines, consultation with HRMS Employee Relations/Labor Relations for counselors who are not meeting these performance standards, etc.).

Impact

- The focus of clinicians has shifted from providing appropriate quality care to primarily concentrating on producing the numbers RCS demands because of fear they will lose their jobs if they don't achieve the visit count expectation.

- Many clinicians work through lunch, don't have breaks, and work overtime without pay to complete all assignments.

- These excessive and unfair performance standards have created an enormous amount of stress which has resulted in a harmful impact on the health and welfare of counselors (i.e., too much stress, burnout, low morale, health issues, depression, seeing a therapist and/or going on a medication protocol, FMLA leave, looking for other employment, retiring early, etc.).

- These negative effects on clinicians have degraded their ability to provide quality care to veterans and their families who deserve better than that, which makes this visit count mandate unethical.

- Most counselors feel that VA/RCS management does not care about them or their well-being.

Sequence of Events

- Summer of 2016: National RCS Director Conference is held in Washington, DC, where numerous VET Center Directors expressed being depressed; some with suicidal ideation. Some stories were shared regarding clinical staff who had committed suicide.

- Since 2016, these issues have been brought to the attention of the RCS leadership numerous times through all five of their districts, but they have not addressed or resolved them.

- July 6, 2017: The RCS District 2 Acting Director (Jeffrey Ferrara) sent an email with another document which explains the quantitative production standards and instructed that productivity performance is to be reviewed weekly by VET Center Team Leaders (Directors), to include the development of action plans for those who do not meet the standards. *This documentation also essentially threatens those who do not meet the quantitative production standards with "accountability consequences" involving HRMS—Labor Relations.*

- August 4, 2017: The RCS District 2 Acting Director (Jeffrey Ferrara) sent an email to his staff where he reiterates how the performance appraisal details how job performance will be measured and rated. He disguises the focus on numbers by referring to it as "translating knowledge, skills and abilities into day-to-day job performance." He then goes on to say those who do not accomplish the expectation should be involved in developing a training plan to help them reach the production goals. He also states this is not a punitive process. However, according to many counselors, it is. *These performance appraisals are solely based on sustaining these quantitative clinical production standards, without any emphasis on quality of care which is what the primary focus should be.*

- September 2017: These concerns were discussed with RCS District 1 Deputy Director Dale Willis at one of the staff meetings during his clinical site visit. He acknowledged he consistently heard the same concerns from other VET Centers he had visited.

- January 18, 2018: I sent an email to RCS Chief Officer Mike Fisher, the RCS District 1 Director Debra Moreno, and RCS District 1 Deputy Directors Dale Willis and Allison Miller, about the negative impact that current clinical productivity standards were having on the health and well-being of counselors, and how this was adversely impacting their ability to provide quality therapeutic services to veterans. Further, I conveyed the ethical dilemma this posed, and offered solutions on how to correct these issues.

- January 25, 2018: After no response to my January 18, 2018, email I forwarded that same email with additional comments to the RCS Chief Officer, all RCS District Directors, all VET Center Directors, and all RCS Counselors throughout the RCS system in order to generate a nationwide RCS open discussion regarding these concerns so this issue could finally be addressed and resolved.

- January 26, 2018, 1:00pm: The RCS Chief Officer responded to everyone in RCS by insinuating there needed to be further discussion to justify these performance standards (i.e., clinical visit counts); without addressing the underlying issue about the negative impact it was having on the health and well-being of clinical staff, and how this was adversely affecting their capacity to provide quality therapeutic services to veterans. He further discouraged continuing this conversation via email, which is the most convenient way for most counselors to do so.

- January 26, 2018, 3:06pm: I responded to the RCS Chief Officer's email and included all RCS District and clinical staff throughout the system. I suggested that email was one of the best ways to continue this discussion since most counselors were not able to be involved in town hall meetings and conference calls because of their over-demanding schedules, which is driven by the expectation to meet the RCS clinical production numbers that is burning out clinicians. I also indicated how it was unreasonable and unrealistic for counselors to continue operating like this and still be able to stay healthy and provide the best quality services to our veterans which they deserve. I urged everyone to voice their concerns, and for both the leadership and clinical staff to come together to resolve this.

- January 26, 2018, 5:40pm: RCS District 1 Deputy Director Dale Willis sent me an email which told me "[T]o cease and desist this email chain communication" and to "respect the chain of command." Subsequently, any communications I had were with RCS counselors only, thereby not breaking chain of command protocol.

- January 26, 2018: I received email responses and/or phone calls from 57 different counselors from 42 VET Centers across 25 states who all conveyed that they and other clinicians at their centers have been negatively impacted by the clinical visit count expectation, which has degraded their ability to provide quality services to veterans (i.e., excessive stress, burnout, poor morale, health issues, depression, having to go on a medication protocol and/or seeing a therapist, time out of work, retiring early, looking for another job, etc.). In separate phone conversations I had with each of these counselors, most of them said they were afraid to speak up because of adverse repercussions they might experience, to include the possibility of losing their job.

- January 27, 2018: I sent a 5-point Likert Scale survey with 11 questions to all RCS counselors across the country in order to assess the degree to which this issue was impacting the health and well-being of clinicians and their capacity to provide quality services to veterans.

- January 29, 2018: The RCS leadership disabled my computer account and subsequently, I received minimal response to the questionnaire which did not allow me to get much input. I only obtained 27 completed surveys (e.g., 12 from District 1, 9 from District 2, 1 from District 3, 3 from District 4, and 2 from District 5). Even though this is not a large enough sample to establish statistical significance in an organization that has over 1,300 counselors, it still has some merit since the results of the survey were consistent with comments made by clinicians, I spoke with who did not do the survey. They mentioned they and their colleagues clearly felt the same as what was reflected in the survey. *There is an obvious trend here that could not be fully exposed due to the RCS leadership not permitting the survey to be completed by telling counselors not to submit it, while disabling my computer access so I could not receive the input.*

- January 29, 2018, 11:23am: RCS District 1 Deputy Director Dale Willis sent my VET Center Director in Providence, RI an email stating that the "survey can have a negative effect and impact on the overall organization," and "Therefore, it was determined this morning that Ted's Outlook access would be discontinued."

- January 29, 2018, 3:45pm: RCS District 1 Director Debra Moreno sent an email to all District 1 staff saying, "this non-sanctioned survey was not vetted, and you are in no way required to respond." Further, she said "In light of the previous discussions regarding the perceived productivity and administrative burdens being placed on counselors, I ask you to not invest time and energy into this survey tool provided it will not be used by RCS leadership in decision making."

- January 29, 2018, 2:10pm: RCS District 2 Director Sarita Figueroa sent an email to all District 2 staff using the exact same wording as the RCS District 1 Director.

- February 1, 2018: An email was sent to all RCS staff throughout the country by Alfred Terriquez, a program support assistant for RCSnet in Colorado, stating that, "RCSnet will be down on Sun, 02/04/2018 at 10:00am-12:00pm (MST) for required maintenance. Users will not be allowed to login to the site during this time. If an employee is already logged in during this timeframe, any work done will not be saved."

- February 1, 2018: I went on extended leave starting 02/01/2018 prior to my official 04/28/2018 retirement date, which was a week earlier than I had intended due to the actions of the RCS leadership to disable my computer account that forced me to leave my job sooner than I wanted, since I could no longer perform my administrative duties without access to a computer.

- February 6, 2018: I was informed by an RCS counselor that all emails generated which contained the survey as an attachment were deleted from everyone's computer account throughout the RCS system. It is suspected that the action taken on February 4, 2018, by RCSnet, as indicated in the above paragraph, was responsible for this occurring.

- February 6, 2018: I filed a complaint with the Office of Special Counsel (OSC) in Washington, DC, since personnel action was taken against me because of whistleblowing and communicating a complaint regarding unfair and unethical practices to the leadership within the Readjustment Counseling Service (RCS), which is part of the Veterans Health Administration (VHA).

- February 16, 2018: The RCS District 2 (Southeast) Acting Director distributed instructions that prohibited VET Center Team Members from sending correspondence, *including emails*, to any non-RCS entities without prior approval of their VET Center Director. This order came out after the series of emails I sent to all directors and clinicians near the end of January 2018 to speak out regarding the adverse impact the clinical visit count expectation was having on the well-being of counselors, which degraded their ability to provide quality services to veterans. *This mandate violates RCS employees' Whistleblower and 1st Amendment Rights of Free Speech, especially since it prevents them from filing legitimate complaints to proper agencies outside of RCS when it is warranted.* This appears to be an obvious attempt by RCS leadership to avoid accountability by using fear tactics to not allow anyone in RCS to voice their concerns to appropriate organizations about legitimate issues that need to be addressed and rectified.

- March 5, 2018: I filed a grievance with the VA Office of Inspector General (OIG) since the Readjustment Counseling Service (RCS), which is part of the Veterans Health Administration (VHA), has been engaged in unfair and unethical practices involving excessive clinical visit count expectations which has adversely impacted the health and well-being of counselors and degraded their ability to provide quality care to veterans and their families.

What the Research Shows

- A nation-wide study led by Carina Vocisano, associate professor of psychology, was conducted by Southern Connecticut State University between 1996 and 2003 where it was determined that counselors with fewer clients tend to get better results than those with a heavy caseload. Specifically, it was found there was a significant drop in treatment effectiveness when a therapist had a caseload of 25 clients or more per week. This trend was even more dramatic with caseloads of 30 or more per week.

- Another study found that burnout of clinicians is also associated with increased employee turnover and declining organizational performance, and that it is particularly detrimental in terms of quality care and customer service (Hancock, Allen, Bosco, McDaniel, and Pierce, 2011—*Journal of Management*, March 2013, Vol. 39/No. 3, 573-603).

- Other research showed there was greater psychological well-being and job satisfaction among counselors who perceive their organization cares about them, which was strongly related to better performance and less turnover (Knapp, Smith, and Sprinkle, 2017—*Nonprofit and Voluntary Sector Quarterly*, 2017, Vol. 46/No. 3, 652-671; Wright and Bonett, 2007—*Journal of Management*, April 2007, Vol. 33/No. 2, 141-160).

- More evidenced-based findings discovered that treating more clients per week was also identified as predictive of higher burnout rates for military mental health providers (Ballenger-Browning, Schmitz, Rothacker, Hammer, Webb-Murphy, and Johnson, 2011—*Military Medicine*, March 2011, Vol. 176/No. 3, 253-260).

Conclusion

This clearly demonstrates that RCS leadership is being unethical by not following evidence-based practices regarding the well-being of counselors and providing optimal quality care, since their productivity standard exceeds what the research shows to be harmful to both counselors and quality of care.

Their focus has clearly changed from caring for veterans and clinical staff to placing a greater emphasis on making sure that unreasonable production expectations are achieved so they can look good at the expense of veterans' welfare and the counselors who serve them.

RCS has been negligent and incompetent since they have not

addressed these concerns after it has been brought to their attention multiple times over the past couple of years. *They have used fear tactics to prevent RCS staff from speaking up about these issues, and employees have experienced reprisals like I have when they do, which is a violation of the Whistleblower Act and 1st Amendment Rights of Free Speech. They apparently attempted a cover-up by deleting emails within RCSnet having to do with voicing concerns regarding this issue.*

Unless these concerns are properly acknowledged and resolved by RCS leadership, the health and well-being of RCS clinical staff will continue to be negatively affected, as will their decreased ability to provide quality care to veterans.

Recommendations

- RCS leadership needs to be held accountable for any violations of the Whistleblower Act, First Amendment Rights, and/or unfair and unethical business practices, etc.

- A survey similar to what I tried to disseminate should be completed by all RCS counselors to assess how severe and widespread these issues are.

- The RCS quantitative production performance standards need to be modified by decreasing the clinical visit count expectation to a fair and ethical level so that the health and well-being of clinical staff and quality of care for veterans does not continue to suffer.

- Place more emphasis on quality care for veterans and the welfare of clinicians, rather than on the quantitative numbers and production.

- Reward and/or give recognition to counselors for quality-of-care efforts and innovation, instead of bonuses based on performance evaluations which rely on meeting the quantitative clinical production expectations.

- RCS should get feedback from counselors in the field before implementing new policies about clinical functions and procedures.

- Only directors with a clinical background should make decisions involving clinical tasks and operations.

- Hire an RCS Chief Officer and RCS District Directors who have a strong clinical background, since the vast majority of them currently do not have adequate clinical experience, and therefore, are not qualified for their positions.

- VET Centers that have not already unionized should consider doing so by applying through their local bargaining units once they have a simple majority of counselors who agree to this, in order to negotiate not having to be held accountable for these unfair and unethical clinical visit count standards.

- Clinicians who have experienced or witnessed these abuses could contact various agencies or entities to report these violations (i.e., Office of Special Counsel (OSC), VA Office of Inspector General (OIG), Federal Labor Relations Authority (FLRA), US Senators or Congresspersons, Senate or House Committee on Veterans Affairs, ACLU/Federal Lawsuit, Local Bargaining Units, SOCIAL MEDIA, and/or Regular Media—TV, Radio, Newspapers/Magazines, etc.).

CHAPTER 14

Office of Resolution Management (ORM/EEO)

The Department of Veteran Affairs Office of Resolution Management website outlines in its Notice of Rights and Responsibilities guidelines for aggrieved persons:

Aggrieved persons who believe they have been discriminated against on the basis of race, color, religion, sex, national origin, age, disability reprisal or genetic information must consult an EEO counselor prior to filing a complaint in order to try to informally resolve the matter.

An aggrieved person must initiate contact with an EEO counselor within 45 calendar days of the date of the matter alleged to be discriminatory or, in the case of a personnel action, withing 45 calendar days of the effective date of action.

If the alleged matter(s) are beyond the 45-calendar day time limit for contacting an EEO counselor, you will be given an opportunity to provide an explanation of your untimely contact to the EEO counselor.

Guidelines for filing complaints are provided by the EEO(C):

The first step to reporting discrimination for federal employees or applicants is to contact their federal agency's equal employment opportunity (EEO) counselor who will guide employees and applicants through the discrimination *complaint process*. This process will result in a voluntary resolution of the complaint or a final decision issued by the federal agency. At the end of the process, employees or applicants who disagree with an agency's final determination may file an appeal with the EEOC or challenge the decision in federal court.

On April 28, 2018, Ted hired Attorney John P. Malone to represent him in his EEO Informal Mediation Process.

In June of 2018, Ted filed a formal EEO Complaint with the Office of Resolution Management (ORM).

On February 5, 2019, EEO/ORM rendered its final agency decision on Ted's allegations as outlined below:

In determining that a working environment is hostile, factors to consider are the frequency of the alleged discriminatory conduct, its severity, whether it is physical threatening or humiliating, and if unreasonably interferes with an employee's work performance. The Supreme Court has stated that:

"Conduct that is not severe or pervasive enough to create an objectively hostile work environment—an environment that a reasonable person would fine hostile or abusive—is beyond Title VII purview.

We note that harassment must be more than disagreements, interpersonal friction, or commonplace workplace events that merely result in hurt feelings. A showing of discriminatory harassment *must* include discreet comment directed against (the Complainant) or disparate treatment of (him) which supports an inference of discriminatory harassment. Harassment, as the term is used in Title VII cases, refers to more than being "subject to stress." The complainant also must show that the conduct complained of was based on her sex. See, Stahl v. Sun Microsystems, In., 19 F.3d 533, (10th Cir. 1994) (stating that no matter how unpleasant, the nature of a working environment must be due to the plaintiff's protected characteristic to support a hostile environment claim).

Harassment is actionable only if it is sufficiently severe or pervasive to alter the condition of the Complainant's employment. *We do not find that the incidents described in your claim rise to the level of conduct that is sufficiently severe or pervasive to constitute an unlawful hostile work environment. You have therefore failed to establish, by a preponderance of evidence, that you were subjected to unlawful harassment on any basis alleged.*"

CHAPTER 15

OIG & OSC Investigations

On February 6, 2018, Ted filed a complaint with the US Office of Special Counsel (OSC). The OSC returned its findings on July 9, 2018. Details of the complaint and the decision are available on the *Broken Promises* webpage: *www.VAbreakingpromises.com.*

The findings referencing the complaint are summarized below:

RE: OSC File No. MA – 18 p 2074

This letter in response to the complaint you filed with the U.S. Office of Special Counsel (OSC) against the U.S. Department of Veterans Affairs (VA), Readjustment Counseling Service (RCS or agency). In your complaint, you made several allegations, including discrimination and retaliation. OSC has carefully reviewed all the information you submitted to our office. Based on our evaluation of the facts and the law, we have made a preliminary determination to close our file on this matter.

1 Discrimination

In your complaint, you stated that in March 2016 the RCS Acting Chief Officer instituted a quantitative clinical measure to RCS counselors' expected production standard, which mandated the number of patient visits counselors were expected to complete per week. You stated that you began to feel depressed due to the excessive visit count standard. You asserted that the production standard exacerbated your mental health disability, but agency officials failed to initiate any changes to accommodate you.

Please note that OSC generally defers action on allegations of discrimination and reprisal for filing an Equal Employment Opportunity (EEO) complaint in favor of the procedures established in the agencies and the Equal Employment Opportunity Commission (EEOC). Thus, we will take no further action on your allegations of disability discrimination.

2 Retirement

In August 2017, you announced your decision to retire. You stated you decided to retire three years earlier than you had planned because you could no longer function in the unreasonable and unethical work environment caused by the oppressive quantitative visit count. You also announced that you would go on extended leave on February 8, 2018, until your official retirement on April 28, 2018.

Generally, an employee-initiated action, such as retirement, is presumed to be voluntary unless the employee can show that the action was obtained through duress or coercion or show that a reasonable person would have been misled by the agency. In order to overcome the presumption of voluntariness one must prove that the retirement was the product of deception, misinformation, or coercion by the agency. To establish involuntariness on the basis of coercion, an employee must show that the agency imposed the terms of an employee's retirement, the employee's circumstances permitted no alternative but to accept, and those circumstances were the result of improper acts by the agency. This is a demanding legal standard.

Regrettably, a stressful work environment is not enough for the MSPB to find that a retirement was coerced. Dissatisfaction with work assignments, a feeling of being unfairly criticized, or difficult or unpleasant working conditions are generally not so intolerable as to compel a reasonable person to resign or retire.

We understand you believed you had no choice but to retire, and we sympathize with your situation. Unfortunately, based on the case law precedent in this area of the law, we do not believe that we could successfully assert that your retirement was involuntary.

3   Whistleblower Retaliation

You alleged retaliation for emailing agency officials in January 2018 about how productivity standards were negatively impacting the RCS counselors' health and well-being as well as their capacity to provide quality therapeutic services to veterans. You alleged that in retaliation, your computer access was disabled, forcing you to begin your extended leave, VET Center Director Rochelle Fortin interrupted you during a staff meeting and accused you of violating the chain of command, which created a negative tone for the conversation and made staff members uncomfortable. You further asserted that while on extended leave, you were instructed not to go to the VET Center without first calling Dale Willis,

RCS District 1 Deputy Director.

We reviewed your allegations of retaliation which prohibits retaliation for whistleblowing. The elements of a violation of the code are: (1) a protected disclosure of information was made; (2) the accused official(s) (e.g., the proposing or deciding official) had knowledge of the disclosure and the identity of the employee making the disclosure; (3) a covered personnel action was taken; and (4) the protected disclosure was a contributing factor in the personnel action or threat of a personnel action.

Unfortunately, after careful review of the information you provided, we cannot conclude that further inquiry is warranted. A violation of section 2302(b)(8) requires a personnel action under the code. Additionally, an employee must show that his whistleblowing activities contributed to the personnel action.

The findings went on to address Ted's allegations regarding his computer being disabled and management's response to Ted sending out the survey. In addition, his assertions included being invalidated through Ms. Fortin's behavior in a staff meeting, when she falsely implied Ted was a threat to the staff's well-being. Ted also claimed VA/VET Center management isolated him from other staff members.

The findings are summarized:

We do not believe we could successfully assert that the agency's actions were retaliatory.

4 First Amendment Rights

You alleged that the agency violated your First Amendment right to free speech by not allowing you to continue the discussion about the productivity standards.

You also stated that on February 16, 2018, RCS District 2 Acting Director Jeffrey Ferrara distributed a memorandum outlining procedures for issuing official correspondences to all RCS District 2 employees. The memorandum stated that VET Center Team Members were not authorized to issue official VET Center/RCS correspondence to any non-RCS entities without the prior approval of the VET Center Director. You asserted that this memorandum violates RCS employees' First Amendment Rights of Free Speech and their rights to engage in whistleblowing activities because it prevents them from filing legitimate complaints to proper agencies outside RCS.

While a public employee does not relinquish First Amendment rights by virtue of government employment, the interest of the Government as employer in regulating speech of its employees differs significantly from its interest in regulating speech of its citizenry in general. Determining the free speech rights of a public employee requires a balancing of "the interests of the (employee), as a citizen, in commenting upon matters of public concern and the interests of the (Government), as an employer, in promoting the efficiency of the public services it performs through its employees."

Because it was clear by the content of your emails, we believe that your statements were made in your capacity as an RCS employee, and not as a private citizen. Therefore, we cannot find that your concerns about RCS performance standards were protected by the First Amendment, such that the agency would be prohibited from considering such statements in making personnel decisions.

Similarly, we also cannot conclude that the February 16 memorandum violates employees' First Amendment right to free speech. In reviewing the February 16 memorandum, it imposed procedure for "official correspondences." Thus, the memorandum applied to correspondences that RCS employees issued in their capacity as employees, not private citizens. As a result, we have no basis for further inquiry into these allegations.

5 Whistleblower Rights

You alleged that RCS leadership violated employees' rights to engage in whistleblowing activities.

You alleged that the agency violated your rights to engage in whistleblowing activities by not allowing you to continue the discussion about the productivity standards. However, Mr. Willis instructed you to cease and desist communicating about the performance standards on the email chain only, not to cease all communication. You were instructed to continue by using the National RCS VA Pulse page. After you sent out the survey to all RCS counselors, Mr. Willis specifically mentioned that there were concerns about how the conversation was transpiring. Further, our examination of Mr. Willis' instructions revealed no language that could be interpreted to restrict your right to lawfully communicate information which you reasonably believe to evidence the type of misconduct identified above.

You also asserted that the February 16 memorandum violates RCS employees' rights to engage in whistleblowing activities because it prevents them from filing legitimate complaints to proper agencies outside RCS. The February 16 memorandum was not a blanket prohibition on employees; rather, it imposed procedures for "official correspondences." We also cannot conclude that the memorandum contained language that could be interpreted to restrict employees' rights to lawfully disclose any of the misconduct identified above. For these reasons, we cannot conclude that the memorandum constitutes a "nondisclosure policy, form, or agreement." Accordingly, for all the reasons stated above, we have no basis for further inquiry into your complaint.

VA Office of Inspector General (OIG)

The following is taken from the VA OIG website:

The Hotline accepts tips or complaints that, on a select basis, result in reviews of:

- VA-related criminal activity
- Systemic patient safety issues
- Gross mismanagement or waste of VA resources
- Misconduct by senior VA officials

The VA OIG investigates substantial allegations of whistleblower reprisal against employees of VA contractors, grantees, subgrantees, and personal services subcontractors. The VA OIG reports substantiated allegations of reprisal to the employer and VA for corrective action.

OSC's primary mission is to safeguard the merit system by protecting federal employees and applicants from prohibited personnel practices, especially reprisal for whistleblowing.

Prohibited personnel practices (PPPs) are employment-related activities that are banned in the federal workforce because they violate the merit system through some form of employment discrimination, retaliation, improper hiring practices, or failure to adhere to laws, rules, or regulations that directly concern the merit system principles.

OSC has the authority to investigate and prosecute violations of the 14 PPPs:

1 Discrimination

2 Considering Inappropriate Recommendations

3 Coercing Political Activity

4 Obstructing Competition

5 Influencing Withdrawal from Competition

6 Granting Unauthorized Advantage

7 Nepotism

8 Whistleblower Retaliation

9 Other Retaliation

10 Other Discrimination

11 Veterans Preference

12 Violating Rules That Implement a Merit System Principle

13 Imposing Non-disclosure Agreement That Doesn't Allow Whistleblowing

14 Accessing Medical Records in Furtherance of Another PPP

On March 5, 2018, Ted filed an online complaint with the VA Office of Inspector General. The complaint, in part, takes a different approach calling out alleged wrong doers and identifying RCS counselors having the same concerns about the productivity requirements.

He also itemizes his own personal complaints along the lines outlined in the OIG & GAO investigation.

On March 27, 2018, the VA OIG Hotline responded via email:

> The OIG has carefully reviewed the allegations you submitted and determined that the items are related to personnel management and prohibited personnel practices. This matter can typically be addressed by the supervisory chain of command, human resources office, or union representative. Accordingly, we plan to take no further action regarding the submission because the subject matter does not fall within our jurisdiction for redress. You may also contact the Office of Special Counsel (OSC).
>
> Lastly, you may contact the Merit Systems Protection Board (MSPB).

Senator Jack Reed (D-RI) received a response to his letter written to the Department of Veterans Affairs Inspector General regarding the OIG's office having refused to accept and investigate Ted's complaint.

The letter read in part:

> As my staff informed you, the personnel matters raised by Mr. Blickwedel typically are not handled by the OIG as there are other administrative forums. We understand that Mr. Blickwedel has already made inquiries with the appropriate agencies on those issues. Regarding the issues involving the changes in performance metrics, the OIG's Office of Healthcare Inspections staff which is comprised of physicians, nurses, and other healthcare clinicians, reviewed all the material that your

office sent and the information that Mr. Blickwedel initially provided the Hotline. They determined that no additional work by the OIG was warranted as the VA is expected to have productivity standards for healthcare providers.

CHAPTER 16

The VET Center Improvement Act

The VET Center Improvement Act of 2021 directs the VA to annually obtain anonymous feedback from VET Center counselors in an electronic database that cannot be altered by any party. This input will focus on any adverse impact that clinical productivity expectations may have on counselor welfare and quality care for veterans. This legislation further stipulates that the VA will establish an internal working group to monitor this process and provide recommendations to the VA Secretary, along with GAO and Congressional Oversight. The VA Secretary is required to submit a yearly report to Congress which addresses any concerns and all corrective action being taken to resolve these issues.

In March of 2018, Ted met with John Kiernan in Senator Reed's Cranston, RI, office. He reviewed the chronology of events

(Addendum) and handed off supporting documents. Following the meeting Mr. Kiernan forwarded the information to John Nobrega in the senator's DC office.

Ted was interviewed by National Public Radio (NPR) on May 9, 2018.

This interview was the beginning of media attention that would facilitate Ted publicizing his story to keep his whistleblower campaign alive and foster political attention.

Walt Buteau with the local Rhode Island TV station, WPRI, did a story on Ted on April 4, 2018.

Ted forwarded copies of the growing media attention to various politicians and other media outlets.

The *Military Times* reporter Todd South wrote an exhaustive story on Ted on June 21, 2018.

Kiernan & Nobrega kept a watchful eye on the media featuring Ted's story.

On August 21, 2018, a letter signed by Senator Reed (D-RI) and Senator Tester (D-MT) was sent to the GAO requesting an investigation into VA VET Center management's actions.

On October 1, 2019, Walt Buteau of WPRI featured Ted in another broadcast.

In May of 2019, an investigative reporter then with NBC, Rich Gardella, reached out to Ted. He said that he had first seen the *Military Times* article Todd South had written in June 2018. He went on to say he had subsequently spent several months vetting Ted's story.

Ted reached out to Chris Bizzacco in Congressman Cicilline's Rhode Island office, supplying him with documents, which were then forwarded to the congressman's DC office.

On July 23, 2019, Ted sent a letter to the House of Representatives Committee for Veterans Affairs, House Subcommittee for Oversight & Investigations. In this letter he addressed how the productivity standards had negatively impacted clinicians' health, welfare and morale.

He addressed the universal concern clinicians had with degradation of their ability to provide quality care to the veterans.

Ted asked that the subcommittee consider legislation that would decrease the clinical production standards to more reasonable levels with more of a focus on quality care and counselor welfare, rather than emphasizing the achievement of excessive quantitative production numbers.

He also asked the RCS leadership get feedback from counselors in the field before implementing new policies about clinical procedures and operations.

In July 2019, while attending a National Whistleblowers Day event in Washington DC, Ted met with John Nobrega in Senator Reed's Washington office. NBC sent a correspondent and film crew to film Ted entering the senator's office.

On November 3, 2019, NBC featured Ted on the NBC Nightly News.

On November 10, 2019, Ted's crusade was featured on NBC's Today Show.

In March of 2020, Ted was interviewed by a GAO investigator, and her team, and subsequently provided them with updated documents.

When the findings of the GAO were published and the VA had responded to the GAO's findings, Ted wrote his analysis of the VA's response and forwarded them to Reed and Cicilline's offices.

Ted addressed what followed:

In November 2020, Congressman Cicilline's team and Senator Reed's staff apprised me that both the House and Senate Committees on Veterans Affairs were fully engaged in this matter, especially due to the recommendations of the GAO as a result of their investigation, as well as the concerns I raised regarding the VA's response to the GAO report.

At the end of December 2020, one of Senator Reed's key staff members notified me that Senator Reed and Senator Tester co-sponsored Congressional legislation entitled "The VET Center Improvement Act" which incorporated the GAO's recommendations, including my suggestions to resolve this dilemma.

From January to May 2021, Ted monitored the writing of the legislation and participated in editing the draft.

Ted recounted details of his contribution to the editing of the legislation.

I was even given the opportunity to provide feedback on the draft legislation before it would be finalized. A staff member from Congressman Cicilline's office concurred that the House Committee on Veterans Affairs supports the Senate version of the Bill, and that his staff was working closely with Senator Reed's staff and members of the Senate Committee on Veterans Affairs.

During this time, I provided a draft copy of the legislation to an Associate Legislative Director of a major Veteran Service Organization (VSO) in Washington, DC in order to coordinate with other VSO Legislative Directors so they could obtain an endorsement for the bill from their political contacts on Capitol Hill.

In March 2021, Senator Reed's military affairs liaison conveyed to me the committees were getting near agreement on the legislation and that the bill would hopefully be introduced to Congress for a vote within the next few months.

During the fall of 2021 the Senate version (*S. 1944*), identical to that of the House version (*H.R. 3575*), was approved by the

Senate Committee on Veterans Affairs and sent to the Senate floor for markup.

In February of 2022, Ted was informed that the House Committee on Veterans Affairs anticipated acting on the proposed legislation within the next few months.

As of the publication of this book, the legislation is winding its way through Congress. Updates can be found on the following website: *www.congress.gov.*

CHAPTER 17

MEDIA

The media played an integral part in moving Ted's whistleblowing crusade forward. Once the coverage began, the VET Center story *got legs*.

An excerpt from Ted's experience with the media follows:

Additionally, between April 2018 and November 2021, I was interviewed by numerous national, state, and local media organizations about the excessive clinical production mandates of the VA/VET Center program and how this has caused counselor burnout and threatens quality care, as well as the retaliation I experienced from VA/RCS management which created a hostile work environment (e.g., NBC News; *Military Times*; NPR; WPRI TV Channel 12 in Providence, RI; and RI Cable PEG TV).

These broadcasts and associated web articles can be viewed on the links below.

NBC: This NBC interview offers a quick and easy overview of Ted's comprehensive journey speaking Truth to Power.
https://www.nbcnews.com/health/health-care/former-therapist-va-hurting-mental-health-care-combat-veterans-its-n1075781

NBC: This Today Show video highlights veterans' views of what the VET Center was before the changes in productivity standards and what it has become subsequent to the change. Al Batras, who ran the program for twenty years and has since retired, speaks plainly.
https://www.today.com/video/successful-program-for-veterans-with-ptsd-is-being-threatened-73234501561

Military Times: Another well written article that showcases Ted's whistleblower experience.
https://www.militarytimes.com/news/your-military/2018/06/21/crisis-in-counseling-how-va-leadership-is-driving-combat-veteran-counselors-to-burnout/

Military Times: This article addresses the nationwide counselor burnout.
https://www.militarytimes.com/news/your-military/2020/09/28/report-vet-counseling-fixes-needed-to-fight-counselor-burnout/

NPR: Blickwedel says his rising sense of hopelessness about his job began a couple of years ago, when the VET Center Program Management changed the way it measured counselor productivity. In addition to asking counselors to track what percentage of their time they spend with clients, the RCS leadership asked counselors to meet a minimum number of visits per week.
https://www.npr.org/2018/05/09/609653871/veterans-counselors-feeling-overworked?live=1

WPRI TV Channel 12, Providence, RI: The local coverage in this broadcast covers Ted's experience up close and personal.
https://www.wpri.com/news/combat-veteran-counselor-files-complaint-over-quota/

More media coverage from WPRI TV Channel 12, Providence, RI:
https://www.wpri.com/target-12/feds-move-forward-on-ri-whistleblower-s-claim-of-harassment-hostility/
https://www.wpri.com/target-12/feds-investigate-combat-vet-counsel-or-quota-claim/
https://www.wpri.com/target-12/feds-back-smithfield-whistleblowers-claim-of-stressful-counseling-quotas/

WPRI TV Channel 12, Providence, RI: This news interview highlights Congressional legislation sponsored by Senator Reed (D-RI) and Congressman Cicilline (D-RI) which supports Ted's crusade.
https://www.wpri.com/military/ri-whistleblower-prompts-congress-to-consider-more-oversight-of-va/

RI Cable PEG TV, Veterans Information Network:
https://www.youtube.com/PEG TV/VA-VET Center Program Quality Care Being Compromised
https://drive.google.com/file/d/1Z3m-k_NH0AFH7QkSP7XESCbVg1CrIUT0/ view?usp=sharing

Updated media coverage can be accessed at: www.VAbreakingpromises.com

CHAPTER 18

VA VET Center Anonymous Quotes

The quotes below are from VET Center counselors via email in response to Ted's nationwide RCS emails which were sent out on January 25th & 26th 2018. He addressed widespread concerns about the negative impact the clinical visit count mandate was having on the health and well-being of counselors, as well as how it was adversely affecting the quality of care for veterans. The quotes validate the systemic trend of these issues within the VET Center Program. Also, there would have been a greater response, but clinicians are afraid to express their opinions due to fear of reprisals from the VA RCS leadership. Further, other responses were not able to be retrieved due Ted's computer access being terminated shortly after he started this email dialogue. The 33 quotes below are a sample of the replies he received from VET Center counselors in 20 different states. The original emails have been safeguarded to protect the identity of these clinicians, and to prove the authenticity of these quotes in situations where it is necessary.

Alaska

"[Y]ou are 1000% correct, brother, and your email was spot on."

Arizona

"I have been with the VET Center since 2007 and I agree with your statements."

Arkansas

"Amen brother, thank you for shining a light … I agree with so much with what you expressed. Thank you for your courage and service."

California

"I am a vet as well, Desert Shield/Storm, and sadly afraid of retribution from RCS, thus the non-work-related email. Your email was spot on!!!! I have been here since 2010 and have seen a drastic decline of morale. I truly feel it's this Mike Fisher guy who has fucked it all up."

Colorado

"I'm sorry it takes someone who is retiring to identify and voice these concerns. It really says something about RCS culture. Please know that many of us around the country stand with you and support what you are saying."

"Thank you for being brave enough to send this out to everyone. We are experiencing the same issues at our VET Center. Our staff has also brought up multiple concerns regarding quality vs. quantity and morale issues to leadership with nothing being done. I too am leaving the VET Center asap due to my health and morale. Thank you again for speaking up!"

Connecticut

"I'd like to first thank you for showing such understanding and compassion for everyone involved. Your bravery alone models leadership! I applaud you and I feel your pain too ... these straining and unfair practices are overwhelming and quite frankly unethical ... in terms of reciprocity as it relates to the Administration's demand/expectations of our measured outcomes and the effectiveness of our work I echo your concerns and can admit that we as clinicians are experiencing if not presenting to work as symptomatically as the population we provide care and treatment to. Whether or not Administration understands the magnitude of this or even cares is frightening to ponder. I do hope your initiative is seen as a positive and that we are treated more like professionals and evaluated more fairly. I hope they see the need for change too. Change that is not complex, change that is needed, change that will be fair and rewarding. Change that is ethical to practice and not unethical."

Florida

"I have been talking to my peers and wife as a sounding board and we all agree that you truly 'hit the nail on the head.' Over the past two years there has been a clear shift to a business model that is not conducive to optimum care being provided by Vet Center Counselors. There are basic principles of caring for people that care for people and we certainly do not see that demonstrated within the RCS. I trust that your letter will be of benefit to us all in that our leadership will address the concerns you expressed and provide 'readjustments' that are doable and of good common clinical sense verses a business model that may make some look good. Our mission is to take care of the veterans – not play numbers games that drive the staff over the edge as we work to provide care to the vets. I am with you 100% and truly appreciate your speaking out on the behalf of all counselors."

"Your experience is much the same as ours in Florida. Throughout my time at RCS [in May it will be 7 years] our leadership has ruthlessly fixated on productivity numbers, using fear and intimidation to force compliance. It's an unwritten rule in our Region [now District] that anyone opposes this, voices dissent, or otherwise says the wrong thing in meetings will eventually lose their job. It is disheartening to tell you that we work in a culture of fear and there's no sign any of this will change. At the slightest hint of a productivity problem there was always the threat of losing my job. No constructive discussion about how to be successful, and no training, but always threats. In a recent monthly teleconference our Director stated that with the changes from the Accountability Act 'we can do whatever we want and there's nothing the Union can to do stop us.' Many of my colleagues were shocked that she could say such a thing, but given my experience that's how they operate anyway. I have no idea how to fix this ... I am often shocked that it's happening at all."

"I really admire your approach and appreciate the information that you shared. I am a new clinician to the Vet Center. I started on October 2. I come with 7 years military/police trauma experience and over 20 years as a clinical social worker. I am a U.S Veteran, like yourself and have a passion for working with Veterans and active military. When I first started, I was read the clinical expectations and informed if I did not meet these expectations, I would be fired. It just seems ludicrous to welcome a new passionate, excited therapist this way. I have recently joined a private practice part time, because I feel I have to keep my options open and protect myself. I really would like to stay at the Vet Center, but I will not stay if the items that you discussed are not addressed. I am not willing to risk my own self-care, and need and have to be supported by the agency I work for. Thank you again for starting this process and being a voice for people who feel intimidated or fear consequences if they come forward. I have been told to be careful and have met clinicians who have stated that they are afraid to speak out."

"Way to go Ted for speaking what we all feel and believe. I shut up a long time ago when I got thrown under the bus years ago so thank you for this masterpiece. Sad to say I'm sure nothing will change because the light bulb doesn't want to change and management doesn't give 1 iota about us and they never will. We have some great people in this program who are literally dying and other long-term greats who have left. FHG's getting PIP'ed and fired for not meeting the BS numbers quota. We joke and say RCS is getting more VA than the VA itself. I'm counting my years left until I can retire. All my retired friends say heck yeah, go nuclear and send this to Shulkin and the media ... . Get off the numbers approach and focus on mission without threatening to fire staff for not always getting the right amount of beans. My retired peers are 100% with you. Lots of scare tactics. My buddy said this would make a great 60 Minutes media piece to focus not necessarily about the BS quotas but the systemic failure of shit leadership."

"Thank you all who have weighed in on this important discussion. We have far too few opportunities to have this candid of a discussion. It is apparent that e-mail is our main vehicle for reaching all of us."

Georgia

"Your words echo what many of us are thinking and feeling and which unfortunately have fallen on deaf ears with the higher ups. All of us here breathed a sigh of relief when reading this as you made the destructiveness and ignorance of these decisions (and in my opinion, unethical decisions) transparent so hopefully the conversations can now begin. We are going to respond but wanted to send a personal email as well and again express my appreciation for you taking the risk and naming what has needed to be named for a very long time."

Maine

"You are absolutely right. I am one of the 'casualties' of RCS. My symptoms progressed to the point I am on Workman's Comp and have been taken out of clinical work. I too have lost faith in RCS and unfortunately the counseling field. I feel RCS has taught me I will never be enough or do enough, and ultimately, I am disposable."

"Your position of feeling squeezed by quantitative metrics without commensurate investment in clinicians' resilience and professional development is familiar, as is your experience of receiving poor, slow, facile or no response from regional management to concerns raised, acute or chronic. I've been with this Vet Center since '04. As we've shored up some aspects of clinical service, expanded geographically and added to the range of services we offer, there has not been comparable support for our role to keep pace with these increasing demands. I agree that this trend does seem to reflect a basic lack of comprehension for how trauma therapy functions over time and the lifespan of our clients. Systemically, this enacts a form of avoidance and reflects an inadequate commitment to the needs of the citizens we serve. It's a shame these administrative priorities and leadership issues are what is driving you from RCS. Other clinicians, office managers and outreach staff are leaving for the same reasons. SW organizing principles would apply to our collective activism and solidarity but most of us probably feel inundated and intimidated. It's a thrill to read your dismissal of Mr. Fisher's condescending instruction to shunt these issues to a side venue: contain and co-opt."

Massachusetts

"I simply want to thank you for your courage and intellect in writing your thorough note below and choosing to send it out. I hope you won't share this but I too think about early retirement because of the high demand from vets in our large county and my inability to hire more staff to assist all of us in having more reasonable numbers. I'm not ready to 'pull the plug' yet, but wanted to express my similar frustrations and again, just thank you for doing what you did."

New Jersey

"I feel your pain. I dare not hit reply all for our new RCS chain of command is vindictive and harassing. I agree our veterans do not receive the best quality care they could receive … especially since the organization made a move from the decentralized to the centralized. Our District managers micro manage now and have unreasonable requests. Having your notes in within 24 hours or 48 hours is unreasonable. Many times I have to decide whether to complete notes or see another client. I choose to complete the notes now, or we will be reprimanded."

New York

"I support your/others' concerns – the bureaucracy, the VA shadow is growing. I hope the conversation you started will continue."

"I agree with what you've said. We had a Team Leader from h---. for 3 yrs on top of all the stuff coming from regional, etc. Our team feels traumatized. I hope that you are not only heard – because regional seems to be good at saying 'we hear you' – but that things improve. I could go on and on!"

North Carolina

"I have only been with RCS for a little over a year and embroiled in my own complaint with District RCS staff and EEO concerning my workplace issues and Team Director. While I'm sure my current issues probably cannot help your cause or my own pain help reduce yours, it is nice to know I am not alone, so thank you for that, and I hope you too know that you are not alone and are not the only one fighting. I too am planning my departure from RCS, because of the unethical and unprofessional work practices encountered and the feeling that things will never be rectified or changed based on what I have seen so far."

"As a clinician who has worked in the RCS system since 2012, I have seen it change as well. I am currently for sure overwhelmed with all the expectations and can feel my burnout setting in. In addition, I started a medication protocol in September of last year due to not only the work environment and requirements of it. And now as I sit as a MFT and MST counselor in 2018, I am ready to leave because I don't have much more left to give. Most of my days there is no time for lunch and no time for documentation. I have at least quarterly throughout the six years I have worked here, had to come in on a day off so I could play catch up on all the documentation required. I have become frustrated over the past few years at the changes."

Pennsylvania

"I read your email and concerns and I concur completely. I am sorry to hear of your struggles that ultimately have led to your decision to resign, and the VA / RCS will hopefully modify their practices to retain competent clinicians that can provide quality services. But I fear that just as you may believe, the VA / RCS will likely not change unless somehow forced to comply. I came to the VA in 2009 and in addition to the expectations of quantitative rather than qualitative standards, I have had numerous difficulties of a similar nature to what you are describing call attention to policies and practices that are clearly not concerned with clinicians and the quality of care that we provide our deserving vets."

Puerto Rico

"I understand your frustration and agree 100% on your points."

Rhode Island

"As you already heard from others, you summed it up well. It was very clear and thorough. It was great that you offered solutions/suggestions, not just complaints. So maybe they will take you seriously. Don't know what else to say. I hope they listen to you and others, and make changes accordingly. Thanks for being our voice!"

Tennessee

"You've showcased significant trends in the system that can be catastrophic to the life of RCS and those we serve. Thank you so much for your candid assessment. We, as a system, need to review these trends and the impact incurred on RCS, practitioners, the vets and families we serve. I also am a practitioner and have found my focus changing from clinical care to cumbersome bureaucratic record keeping processes as well. We need to rebalance the scale for the life of our system, practitioners and the vets we serve!"

"[W]e too experienced a portion of the backlash from district for speaking up against for how they have treated us and what we think has negatively impacted our Veterans and ourselves. We have tried talk with our leadership fairly and rationally to inform how their processes negatively impact our client care and ourselves. But it has fallen on deaf ears. We wish to keep our jobs so we can continue to serve Veterans. Thus, we are waiting for another time and other avenues to attempt to reason with district and national offices. It has been a long hard road and it is not over yet. However, with people like you speaking up that gives all hope that positive change can occur. If you decide to go forth in this effort and are seeking other avenues to get national/ district to change their standards, please let us know so we can support that effort. I just wished the leadership could see what they these processes are doing to our morale and more importantly to the veterans. What happen to a friendly and relaxed atmosphere that is written in our mission? It is consumed with protecting our jobs by packing our schedules, over committing our time and writing long emails and documentation for fear of losing our jobs. All of this focus on numbers is covertly and overtly creating an atmosphere that is contrary to this very mission. We are saturated with emails, required staffing supervision and repetitive documentation that takes away from being available for our veterans. I cannot tell you the number of veterans that have been coming to the vet center for years that have stopped coming because of the 'impersonal indifference' that they have felt from our leadership. These similar comments were said by our own Vietnam veterans after our regional director spoke at a town hall meeting. She simply didn't get it and it showed. Know you are speaking for many!"

"I've just read through your e-mail put out this week showcasing the concerns brought about by the productivity changes. I just returned from a one-month FMLA sabbatical this past December as I needed time off before I was due to burn out. In that time off I sought and successfully garnered a trusted therapist, an adjustment on my medications and twice a week yoga and meditation sessions. Those tools have helped some but first I had to put the brakes on my career in order to get access to them. I do agree that 85% is an extremely high percentage of "success." In my 20 years of serving in the Army National Guard and in all of my PME schools and courses, I've never had a testing standard set so high for success."

Vermont

"I cannot tell you how validating it is for me to read this, and see your courage in speaking to it openly. I am resigning my position. I have never given up, but now I am because, the unsustainable culture keeps me from being focused in my sessions, I am not sleeping and I cannot help my Vets to the degree they need."

Virginia

"I am reaching out to you as we have had our union involved in the quantitative measures in our performance evaluations and it has remained back to the old standards of the prior performance evaluations. I cannot share a lot. I am concerned and worried about speaking out and give you all much kudos for doing so as our mouths are now shut here. Thank you for your words and emails. It made us feel united with others here."

"I'm with you, but I don't know what else we can do. I've been with the Vet Center for a little over 6 years and am surprised by the negative changes I've seen happen so quickly. The vets are paying the price as are we as therapists. Thanks for speaking up."

"Again, thank you so much for your sad, but true assessment. I find it interesting that a bureaucracy that demands so much from its constituents provide so little support. It's difficult to deliver consistent, focused, quality care to Veterans, when the quantity of Clients appears to be more important than purpose of the organization. It's been said that, 'the squeaky wheel gets the grease;' and I truly believe it. I really appreciate you Ted for speaking out and I hope this protest brings positive change for our Veterans that we service, as well as Vet Center Clinicians, Admin staff, Directors and RCS as a Whole."

"I am new to RCS (September 2017) and I've observed all of the items that you have mentioned. All items are valid and thank you for speaking the truth."

Utah

"Your letter was beautifully written and expressing something that all of us are struggling with. I am hoping that your letter and (all of) our concerns, and how we are going to respond to these issues, will be discussed at our staff meeting next week and that some real improvements happen. You are my hero. Let me know what I can do to help. I thought that your suggestions were great. If you didn't get an outpouring of response, know that it is because we are scurrying around with our 7 appointments a day."

CHAPTER 19

Lessons Learned

On January 26, 2018, F. Joshua McCumber, EdS, MHA, Licensed Marriage and Family Therapist, Licensed Mental Health Counselor, Gainesville VET Center, sent an email further outlining the ramifications associated with the negative impact that quantitative clinical performance expectations have had on RCS clinicians.

> I would like to take this opportunity to thank Ted Blickwedel for his thoughts on the culture of RCS and the need for change, as well as those brave enough to respond with comments of support. I hope more staff will add their voices and contribute to a dialogue across our organization. I have been within RCS since '12 and know of similar concerns in my region and zone. For my contribution to this dialogue, I would like to echo Ted's concerns using references from the professional literature. Other organizations and industries have figured these challenges out and identified the dysfunction that we are all experiencing.

RCS needs to recognize that employee turnover is a valid indicator of organizational performance. Voluminous research suggests that increased turnover has a negative effect on human and social capital, disrupts operations and collective function, and saddles remaining staff with newcomer orientation and training (Hancock, Allen, Bosco, McDaniel, and Pierce, 2011). In terms of RCS, we not only lose an employee, but a highly-trained clinician with VA specific tacit organizational knowledge, not to mention highly specialized understanding of combat trauma culture and treatment. Human and social capital losses associated with turnover have been found to outweigh the potentially functional effects in a variety of industry contexts (Hancock, Allen, Bosco, McDaniel, and Pierce, 2011).

What I find particularly salient are inquiries that have elucidated the relationship that exists between turnover and declining organizational performance and how it is particularly detrimental in terms of customer service, quality, and safety measures than for other performance metrics that were investigated (Hancock, Allen, Bosco, McDaniel, and Pierce, 2011). Also, the cost of employee replacement has been estimated at 1.5–2.5 times the annual salary of the incumbent job holder, pointing to a potentially significant financial impact from employee turnover as well (as cited in Wright and Bonett, 2007). It may be intuitive that employee psychological well-being as well as job satisfaction are strongly correlated with employee turnover, but research suggests that psychological well-being and job satisfaction are correlated with job performance as well (Wright and Bonett, 2007). In other words, a valued employee in an organization invested in his/her psychological well-being will be more fulfilled in his/her roles and consistently perform better – especially in terms of customer service, quality, and safety. And, that employee will stay.

Knapp, Smith, and Sprinkle (2017) looked at how perceptions of job characteristics (e.g., autonomy, feedback, skill variety, task identity) and perceptions of organizational support (i.e., whether employees believe that their organization values their contributions and cares about their individual well-being) impact job satisfaction, employee outcomes, and turnover intentions. Perceptions of organizational support was identified as an important and consistent predictor of job satisfaction and turnover intentions. Job characteristics, except for autonomy, exhibited limited predictive validity for job satisfaction and turnover intentions (Knapp, Smith, and Sprinkle, 2017). In other words, organizations that allow autonomy and communicate the value of the employees' contributions (i.e., employee engagement), have better performance and less turnover.

When mental health professionals leave organizations, detrimental effects on quality of care is reflected in the literature as well. Let's look closer at predictors of turnover among mental health professionals. Reasons for leaving include incivility at work with colleagues and supervisors, lack of autonomy, perceptions of unfair treatment, feeling psychologically unsafe at work, and emotional exhaustion (Yanchus, Periard, and Osatuke, 2017).

Burnout has been defined as a psychological syndrome that develops in response to chronic emotional and interpersonal stress and is characterized by emotional exhaustion, depersonalization, and feelings of ineffectiveness or lack of personal accomplishment. Burnout is separate from compassion fatigue which is typically conceptualized to be a unique occupational hazard for those working with traumatized clients and has symptoms similar to PTSD (Thompson, Amatea, and Thompson, 2014). Predictors of burnout for mental health practitioners are largely work environment-related; specifically, perceptions of coworker and supervisor support, perceptions of fairness, and perceptions of support from the organization (Yanchus, Periard, and Osatuke, 2017). Treating more clients per week was also identified as predictive of higher burnout rates for military mental health providers (Ballenger-Browning, Schmitz, Rothacker, Hammer, Webb-Murphy, and Johnson, 2011).

It is important for organizations to monitor perceptions of staff and collect employee feedback on aspects of the mental healthcare delivery workplace and translate findings into corrective action at the direct supervisor level (Yanchus, Periard, and Osatuke, 2017). I describe this process simply as bottom-up feedback and employee engagement. For the literature summary above, I spent approximately 45 minutes searching for articles in a database. It was not hard to do and the articles were not hard to find. The point I would like to make is that there is an abundance of knowledge in professional articles and journals. I do not believe our professional dissociation within RCS is a matter of the VHA and RCS being too large and unique that we haven't found a solution. It just takes the right prioritization of workplace values, courage, and great leadership (which is different than management).

References

Ballenger-Browning, K. K., Schmitz, K. j., Rothacker, J. A., Hammer, P.S., Webb-Murphy, J. A., and Johnson, D. C. (2011). "Predictors of burnout among military mental health providers." *Military Medicine. 176, 253-260.*

Hancock, J. I., Allen, D. G., Bosco, F. A., McDaniel, K. R., and Pierce, C. A. (2011). "Meta-analytic review of employee turnover as a predictor of firm performance." *Journal of Management. 39, 573-603.*

Knapp, J. R., Smith, B. R., and Sprinkle, T. A. (2017). "Is it the job or the support? Examining structural and relational predictors of job satisfaction and turnover intention for non-profit employees." *Nonprofit and Voluntary Sector Quarterly. 46, 652-671.*

Thompson, I. A., Amatea, E. S., and Thompson, E. S. (2014). "Personal and contextual predictors of mental health counselors' compassion fatigue and burnout." *Journal of Mental Health Counseling. 36, 58-77.*

Wright, T. A., and Bonett, D. G. (2007). "Job satisfaction and psychological well-being as nonadditive predictors of workplace turnover." *Journal of Management. 33, 141-160.*

Yanchus, N.J., Periard, D., and Osatuke, K. (2017). "Further examination of predictors of turnover intention among mental health professionals." *Journal of Psychiatric and Mental Health Nursing, 24, 41-56.*

Ted Blickwedel: I learned many lessons during the course of this advocacy campaign which are important to share so those who are compelled to undertake similar crusades can enhance their chances of a favorable outcome. These useful and indispensable guidelines are outlined below and will help advance more potential for an effective effort and successful result.

1   It is essential that the consequences of any unethical and harmful conduct being reported, to include retaliation, is well documented through written material, recordings, witnesses, and/or relevant research that validates the allegations. This kind of evidence is critical to establish credibility.

2   Solicit support from as many colleagues and peers as possible to back your activist endeavor since there is strength in numbers when you are on a united front, both for the cause and your emotional sustenance. However, realize that most coworkers and associates will be afraid to stand with you because of fear of reprisals. This is typical due to reacting out of survival instincts to protect themselves, so try not to take it personally.

3   Enlist assistance from family and friends to serve as confidantes and a source of encouragement, especially during difficult times in the process to help maintain a healthy and balanced mental state.

4   Your own self-care cannot be stressed enough. This was my greatest downfall, particularly early on as I described previously, due to allowing myself to be too overwhelmed which resulted in my physical and emotional demise that led to my pulmonary embolism which almost killed me. It is very important to have good nutrition, engage in relaxing and enjoyable activities, exercise regularly, and seek counseling or therapy if necessary. Specifically, I recommend Qi Gong, Yoga, Meditation, Therapeutic Massage, and/ or other suitable practices to build and sustain physical, mental, emotional, and spiritual resilience. This will help immensely to

206

more easily navigate through and cope with the challenging stress generated by activism and the toxic retaliation tactics that usually go along with it.

5   Get organizational assistance from a reputable establishment that is knowledgeable and experienced with whistleblowing and its ramifications prior to forging ahead with your initiative. This is something I neglected at the beginning, but I did not know this was available until someone referred me to Whistleblowers of America (WoA) shortly after I started my advocacy campaign. WoA is a nonprofit organization devoted to providing peer-to-peer mentor support for those who are in the process of reporting unethical conduct of their federal employers, so they can understand retaliation tactics that are used against them and develop strategies to help them effectively manage this course of action. Jackie Garrick, who is the founder and CEO of WoA, is also actively involved with members of Congress in Washington, DC, to promote legislation that will enhance whistleblower support and protection. Her website, *www.whistleblowersofamerica.org*, provides more details and other useful information about this (e.g., resources, news and press releases, and testimonials). I strongly endorse Jackie and her organization which were extremely helpful to me. Further, my blog is displayed on the WoA website where comments can be posted at the following link: *https://whistleblowersofamerica.org/2018/12/12/vet-center-quality-care-and-counselor-welfare-issues/*

6   Obtaining media coverage to raise awareness and getting the backing of politicians and/or other influential entities is crucial in order to successfully achieve your objectives and produce authentic change that is truly beneficial. This will also potentially foster significant momentum which can be motivating and inspiring to keep pushing forward.

7   Develop grassroots relationships and support with colleagues, family, friends, and centers of influence who are willing to get

directly involved with your efforts or at least assist in spreading the word and promoting appropriate action regarding your ongoing campaign through emails, social media, and contacting their Congressional Delegates to endorse your endeavor.

8 Stay connected with your support network and keep them updated to maintain their interest and involvement.

9 Exhibit a professional, tactful, and composed demeanor throughout all your interactions with media contacts, politicians, other supporters, and adversaries. It is vital, too, to be organized, clear, and succinct with what you say and how you articulate your message. This will help facilitate greater receptiveness to what you are communicating.

10 Be positive and have hope in what you are doing because of knowing it is possible to effect genuine and constructive change against what appears to be insurmountable odds when others before you have demonstrated it can be done.

Conclusion

The consequence of the VET Center Program's unreasonable clinical production metrics and excessive administrative workload policies that have been forced on counselors, combined with a shortage of clinicians, high caseloads, and increased counselor turnover rates, prevent veterans from getting adequate services they deserve, and especially puts suicidal veterans at higher risk. This is further harmful to the health, welfare, and morale of clinicians who take care of our veterans. Therefore, corrective action is desperately needed to transform the dysfunctional VA/RCS system that is more concerned with quantitative productivity rather than counselor well-being and quality of care for our veterans and their families.

It is imperative that clinical performance standards and other administrative requirements be continually monitored through GAO and Congressional oversight, in accordance with the GAO recommendations in their report (*https://www.gao.gov/products/GAO-20-652*), so adjustments can be made to ensure quality care and counselor welfare is not compromised. This should be augmented by an internal RCS working group to examine this, along with anonymous feedback from counselors in the field through a protected database, as proposed by pending *Congressional legislation*. Otherwise, the health and well-being of clinical staff will continue to suffer which will hurt their ability to deliver quality care, and this will result in veterans and their families not receiving sufficient quality services they deserve. This will also allow less emphasis on achieving excessive quantitative production numbers which only serves the bureaucratic system instead of the veterans we are here to help. The VA/VET Center program management must be held accountable for this and for retaliation against employees who speak up to address these issues.

Overall, this is why clinical visit count and performance standards must be maintained at a reasonable and ethically compliant level in the VA/VET Center program with a greater emphasis on quality care and counselor well-being. Concurrently, approving and allocating adequate Congressional funding to hire more clinical staff is necessary in order to meet the demand for services and reduce excessive caseloads. Finally, strong legislation to support and protect whistleblowers needs to be passed by Congress which sponsors severe consequences for those who retaliate against them.

ADDENDUM

Chronology of Events

- **March 1, 2016:** The RCS Acting Chief Officer, Charles Flora, instituted another quantitative clinical measure that was added to the expected production standard, which mandated the number of visits a counselor was supposed to have. It was computed by multiplying hours worked by 1.5 and dividing this by 2, which resulted in the total expected visits a counselor should have. This figure was then divided into the number of actual visits that gave you a percentage that is the proportion of actual visits to total expected visits. The overall visit count expressed as this percentage was expected to be between 85% and 100%. This basically equated to counselors being required to spend 25.5–30 hours per week with clients in a 40-hour work week (i.e., 25.530 visits per week considering the industry standard is 50-60 minutes per session).

- **Summer of 2016:** The National RCS Director Conference in Washington, DC, was held where numerous VET Center directors expressed being depressed, some with suicidal ideation. There were even some stories shared regarding clinical staff who had committed suicide. This was conveyed at a staff meeting by the Warwick VET Center Director, Rochelle Fortin.

- **During and beyond 2016:** The issue of the excessive RCS clinical visit count production mandate was brought to the attention of the VET Center leadership numerous times through all 5 of their districts, but they had not addressed or resolved this.

- **August 2016:** I began to feel very depressed because I was no longer able to provide quality care for veterans due to the excessive pressure of the clinical visit count standard being enforced by RCS (i.e., having to choose "producing the numbers" over quality of care in order to protect my job).

- **September 2016:** I was required by my VET Center Director, Rochelle Fortin, to complete a Performance Improvement Plan via email since I did not meet the clinical visit count expectation, in spite of my best efforts to do so. This PIP was forwarded by Ms. Fortin to the RCS District 1 office, which resulted in my experiencing significant duress that further exacerbated my depression.

- **October 14, 2016:** I had an appointment at the *PVAMC* (Providence VA Medical Center) with a psychologist due to my depression being triggered by work-related stress, which made me feel more hopeless with increased irritability and insomnia.

- **October 28, 2016:** I had an appointment at the PVAMC with a psychiatrist since my depression had become significantly worse during the past couple months as a result of the bureaucratic-induced stress in the work place referenced above, which started me thinking that I might have to leave my job because of my declining ability to provide quality care to veterans due to the excessive clinical visit count mandate which was forcing me to be more concerned about quantitative production instead of quality service.

- **November 2016:** My depression had escalated to severe with increased suicidal ideation, which was the worse it has ever been. This made it more difficult for me to adequately perform my job, which caused me to take time off from work and isolate at home due to my mood being more negatively impacted. I reported all this to my psychiatrist during my appointment with him on November 25, 2016. He subsequently increased the dosage on my depression and anxiety medication. During a supervision session with VET Center Director Rochelle Fortin, I explained what was going on with me. She mentioned she was concerned about me and recommended that I take time off if I needed to.

- **December 2016:** Via email, Rochelle Fortin cancelled a supervision appointment we had scheduled due to a last-minute conflict, but she did not reschedule it with me. I started to think she did not want to be bothered with me, and I began to feel that maybe I did not belong at the VET Center anymore. I had an appointment with my psychiatrist on December 19, 2016, since I was still very depressed and feeling exceedingly more irritable. Once again, he increased the dosage on my depression and anxiety medication.

- **January 27, 2017:** I had an appointment with my psychiatrist at the PVAMC since I was still very depressed and significantly irritable, as well as having problems taking care of myself. At this point, I was also starting to isolate from family members and had to take more time off from work the previous month. Further, my suicidal ideation had escalated.

- **February 2017:** I approached Ms. Fortin to setup another supervision session with her since she had not attempted to reschedule the one she cancelled in December. Later this same month, I finally met with Ms. Fortin for supervision and I asked her if she was aware that she had not once in the last few months checked in with me to see how I was doing. After she failed to acknowledge this, I felt awkward and began to minimize it by saying to her, "I know you have a lot on your plate and it is easy to get sidetracked." Then the subject abruptly changed and did not really get addressed. On February 24, 2017, I had an appointment with my psychiatrist because I was still very depressed, irritable, and feeling extremely hopeless. Additionally, my lack of interest in everything and anything had increased, and I was feeling a lot of guilt since my capacity to provide quality services to veterans had diminished due to anxiety about not meeting the RCS clinical visit count expectation. Subsequently, another depression medication was added to my treatment protocol.

- **March 17, 2017:** I had a C&P (Compensation & Pension) exam with a psychologist at the Jamaica Plains, MA VAMC. He concluded that the symptoms of my psychological state had a significant and negative impact on my ability to function at my job, which was triggered by work-related stress. He also inferred that my symptoms and impairment were currently a lot more severe, frequent, and numerous when compared to my past history.

- **July 6, 2017:** The RCS District 2 Acting Director, Jeffrey Ferrara, sent an email with another document which explained the quantitative production standards, and instructed that productivity performance was to be reviewed weekly by VET Center Team Leaders (directors), to include the development of action plans for those who were not meeting the standards. This documentation also essentially threatened those who did not meet the quantitative production standards with "accountability consequences" involving HRMS/Labor Relations.

- **August 4, 2017:** The RCS District 2 Acting Director, Jeffrey Ferrara, sent an email to his staff where he reiterated how the performance appraisal spelled out how job performance would be measured and rated. He disguised the focus on numbers by referring to it as "translating knowledge, skills and abilities into day-to-day job performance." He then went on to say those who did not accomplish the expectations would be involved in developing a training plan to help them reach the production goals. He also stated this was not a punitive process. However, according to a large number of counselors, it was. These performance appraisals were solely based on sustaining the quantitative clinical production standards, without any emphasis on quality of care, which is what the primary focus should have been.

- **August 2017:** I announced to the staff at the end of this month that I decided to retire 3 years earlier than I had planned because I could no longer function in this unreasonable and unethical work environment due to the oppressive quantitative visit count metrics that were impeding my ability to provide quality care to veterans. I conveyed to them how this had caused me to have severe depression over the past year. I explained, too, that I intended to go on extended leave starting February 8, 2018, until my official retirement date of April 28, 2018. I let it be known that I would not be able to take on any new clients since I had to start the termination process with my case load of 71 veterans in the near future. I specified I would not be doing any new assessments or seeing old clients that might desire to resume therapy, due to not wanting to establish any connections with anyone while winding down my case load.
- **September 2017:** The concerns regarding the excessive clinical visit count mandate was discussed with RCS District 1 Deputy Director Dale Willis at one of our staff meetings during his clinical site visit. He acknowledged he consistently heard the same concerns from other VET Centers he had been to.
- **December 2017:** I felt pressured, anxious and guilty, which triggered feelings of depression when my VET Center Director, Ms. Fortin, asked me if I would be interested in doing a couple of assessments. I had explained to her and other staff members a few months earlier that I would not be able to do this while trying to terminate with clients.
- **January 18, 2018:** I sent an email to RCS Chief Officer Mike Fisher, RCS District 1 Director Debra Moreno, and RCS District 1 Deputy Directors Dale Willis & Allison Miller, about the negative impact that current clinical productivity standards were having on the health and well-being of counselors, and how this was adversely impacting their ability to provide quality therapeutic services to

215

veterans. I conveyed the ethical dilemma this posed and offered solutions on how to correct this. I sent this email because the RCS leadership failed to address these issues after it had been brought to their attention numerous times during the past year-and-a-half through the normal chain of command.

- **January 25, 2018:** After no response to my 01/18/2018 email, I forwarded that same email with additional comments to the RCS Chief Officer, all RCS District directors, all VET Center directors, and all RCS counselors throughout the RCS system in order to generate a nationwide RCS open discussion regarding these concerns so this issue could finally be addressed and resolved.

- **January 26, 2018, 1:00pm:** The RCS Chief Officer responded to everyone in RCS by insinuating that there needed to be further discussion to justify these performance standards (i.e., clinical visit counts), without addressing the underlying issue about the negative impact it was having on the health and well-being of clinical staff, and how this was adversely affecting their capacity to provide quality therapeutic services to veterans. He further discouraged continuing this conversation via email, which is the most convenient way for most counselors to communicate with each other.

- **January 26, 2018, 3:06pm:** I responded to the RCS Chief Officer's email and included all RCS District and clinical staff throughout the system. I suggested email was one of the best ways to continue this discussion since most counselors were not able to be involved in town hall meetings and conference calls because of their over-demanding schedules, which is driven by the expectation to meet the RCS clinical production numbers that is burning out clinicians. I also indicated how it was unreasonable and unrealistic for counselors to continue operating like this and still be able to stay healthy and provide the best quality services to our veterans. I urged everyone to voice their concerns and for both the leadership and clinical staff to come together to resolve this.

- **January 26, 2018, 5:40pm:** RCS District 1 Deputy Director Dale Willis sent me an email telling me "To cease and desist this email chain communication" and to "respect the chain of command." Subsequently, any communications I had were with RCS counselors only, thereby not breaking chain of command protocol.

- **January 26, 2018:** I had received email responses and/or phone calls from 57 different counselors from 42 VET Centers across 25 states who all conveyed they and other clinicians at their centers had been negatively impacted by the clinical visit count expectation, degrading their ability to provide quality services to veterans (i.e., excessive stress, burnout, poor morale, health issues, depression, having to go on a medication protocol and/or seeing a therapist, time out of work, retiring early, looking for another job, etc.). In separate phone conversations I had with each of these counselors, most of them said they were afraid to speak up because of adverse repercussions they might experience, to include the possibility of losing their job.

- **January 27, 2018:** I sent a 5-point Likert Scale survey with 11 questions to all RCS counselors across the country in order to assess the degree to which this issue was impacting the health and well-being of clinicians and their capacity to provide quality services to veterans.

- **January 29, 2018:** The RCS leadership disabled my computer account. I received minimal response to the questionnaire which did not allow me to get much input. I only obtained 27 completed surveys (e.g., 12 from District 1, 9 from District 2, 1 from District 3, 3 from District 4, and 2 from District 5). Even though this is not a large enough sample to establish statistical significance in an organization that has over 1,300 counselors, it still has some merit because the results of the survey were consistent with comments made by clinicians I spoke with who did not do the survey. They mentioned that they and their colleagues clearly felt the same as what was reflected in the survey. So, there is an obvious trend here that could not be fully exposed due to the RCS leadership not permitting the survey to be completed by telling counselors not to submit it, while disabling my computer access so I could not receive the input. Therefore, it should be noted what the questionnaire uncovered.

- **January 29, 2018, 11:23am:** RCS District 1 Deputy Director Dale Willis sent my VET Center Director in Providence, RI an email stating the "survey can have a negative effect and impact on the overall organization," and "Therefore, it was determined this morning that Ted's Outlook access would be discontinued."

- **January 29, 2018, 3:45pm:** The RCS District 1 Director Debra Moreno sent an email to all District 1 staff saying, "this non-sanctioned survey was not vetted and you are in no way required to respond." She stated, "In light of the previous discussions regarding the perceived productivity and administrative burdens being placed on counselors, I ask you to not invest time and energy into this survey tool provided it will not be used by RCS leadership in decision making."

- **January 29, 2018, 2:10pm:** The RCS District 2 Director Sarita Figueroa sent an email to all District 2 staff using the exact same wording as the RCS District 1director.

- **January 31, 2018:** Ms. Fortin agreed that I could address the staff at our meeting this same day in order to have a positive closure due to my near-term departure, and also to help dissolve any divisiveness that might exist since a couple of staff members were uncomfortable with the emails I sent to the RCS leadership which discussed the clinical visit count mandate issue. At the staff meeting, while trying to facilitate this process in a constructive way, Ms. Fortin interrupted and accused me of violating the chain of command which was not relevant to the dialogue. This intrusion created a negative tone for the conversation that made staff members uncomfortable and did not allow enough time for a proper completion. Another opportunity to accomplish this was never granted by Ms. Fortin. This incident left me feeling invalidated and betrayed, which triggered my depression to the point where I was having suicidal ideation because of feeling worthless and that I did not belong.

- **February 1, 2018:** I spoke with Ms. Fortin in the morning to express how hurt I felt by what she did the previous day (i.e., invalidated, betrayed, etc.). I also told her that, although I trusted her professionally, I could no longer trust her personally because of how she sabotaged my effort to have a positive closure with the staff before my departure. All she said to me was, "Ted, I don't know what you want me to say." During this exchange she never acknowledged or seemed to care how all of this affected me, which made me feel even more wounded and depressed. Other staff members mentioned to me they were disappointed by what she did and that it was not fair to me.

- **February 1, 2018:** An email was sent to all RCS staff throughout the country by a program support assistant for RCSnet in Colorado. Alfred Terriquez stated that, "RCSnet will be down on Sun, 02/04/2018 at 10:00am-12:00pm (MST) for required maintenance. Users will not be allowed to login to the site during this time. If an employee is already logged in during this timeframe, any work done will not save."

- **February 1, 2018:** I went on extended leave starting February 1, 2018, prior to my official April 28, 2018 retirement date, which was a week earlier than I had intended due to the actions of the RCS leadership to disable my computer account, forcing me to leave my job sooner than I wanted because I could no longer perform my administrative duties without access to a computer.

- **February 6, 2018:** I was informed by an RCS counselor that all emails generated which contained the survey as an attachment were deleted from everyone's computer account throughout the RCS system. It is suspected that the action taken on February 4, 2018 by RCSnet, as indicated in the above paragraph, was responsible for this occurring.

- **February 6, 2018:** I filed a complaint with the Office of Special Counsel (OSC) in Washington, DC since personnel action was taken against me because of whistleblowing and communicating a complaint regarding unfair and unethical practices to the leadership within the Readjustment Counseling Service (RCS), which is part of the Veterans Health Administration (VHA).

- **February 7, 2018:** I forwarded a letter I wrote via email to a colleague at work who read it to everyone at the staff meeting. I did this because I was not given the opportunity by Ms. Fortin to have the proper closure with everyone before my departure. I was previously informed by other staff clinicians they felt the same way, and that it was not complete for them either. I was also told by some staff members later that Ms. Fortin had made the following comments at the staff meeting at different times after my letter was read: *"When I came into work this morning I was looking around since I thought Ted could be lurking around somewhere." "Ted knows where we all live," "Ted is very precise and calculating."* Additionally, a couple of staff members mentioned to me that on another day Ms. Fortin made a statement near my office, which was apparently unlocked, by saying, *"I thought Ted's office was locked when he left. I wouldn't be surprised if he made extra keys before he departed."* One of the staff members responded to her by suggesting it was probably the house cleaning personnel who gained access to his office. These same two staff members acknowledged they thought Ms. Fortin was trying to further distance me from her and the staff by perpetuating false fears about me that had no basis in any fact. They further agreed she was doing this because of actually being afraid of how my communication with the RCS leadership would reflect on her (i.e., protecting her own skin by *trying to throw me under the bus*). They also said there are now a number of staff members who do not trust her after observing how she unfairly treated me without just cause, in order to protect herself at my expense.

- **February 8, 2018:** I received an email from RCS District 1 Deputy Director Dale Willis that ambiguously stated Ms. Fortin needed a break, but not specifying why. He suggested that a "time out" might be the best for everyone (e.g., which currently appears to myself and others to have been a delaying tactic to covertly not allow me to have access to the VET Center or the staff so I could have appropriate closure with everyone, which Ms. Fortin was afraid of because of what was explained above). He insinuated the staff was also requesting this, when in fact most of them I spoke with did not feel this way. This blatant attempt to dismiss and isolate me caused my depression and suicidal ideation to increase, which resulted in more agitation, worse sleep disturbance, and further isolation. I sat home and did nothing.

- **February 16, 2018:** The RCS District 2 (Southeast) Acting Director distributed instructions that prohibited VET Center Team Members from sending correspondence, including emails, to any non-RCS entities without prior approval of their VET Center director. This order came out after the series of emails I sent to all directors and clinicians near the end of January 2018 to speak out regarding the adverse impact the clinical visit count expectation was having on the well-being of counselors, which degraded their ability to provide quality services to veterans. This mandate violates RCS employees' Whistleblower and 1st Amendment Rights of Free Speech because it prevented them from filing legitimate complaints to proper agencies outside of RCS, even when it is warranted. This appeared to be an obvious attempt by RCS leadership to avoid accountability by using fear tactics to not allow anyone in RCS to voice their concerns to appropriate organizations about legitimate issues that needed to be addressed and rectified.

- **February 20, 2018**: I sent an email to some staff members thanking them for being supportive of what I was going through. I informed them Dale Willis had told me that Ms. Fortin refused to have a meeting with him and I due to "still needing some distance" (e.g., which was just another attempt on her part to not be accountable for how she was treating me, which further compounded my depression. I also stated to them how not being allowed to have a voice in all this would further isolate me, and that I was extremely distraught about this and could not take it anymore.

- **February 20, 2018:** A staff member responded to my email referenced above and indicated that having a farewell celebration for me would be in order sooner rather than later. This staff member also went on to say that "I do not feel that you threatened anyone nor broke the chain of command in any way." My colleague also mentioned "It would have been nice if the staff could have presented their positive sentiments to you publicly for your tremendous contribution to the veterans, VET Center, and staff."

- **February 22, 2018:** Ms. Fortin called me at home. I mentioned I would like to have a meeting with her, but she said she was not ready for that without specifying why. I also stated how I noticed her demeanor had changed after I expressed my disappointment to her on February 1st about how she handled the January 31st staff meeting when she invalidated me and upended my efforts to have a positive closure with the staff before my departure. I conveyed to her that she may not be aware of how this hurt me, but she did not respond to that. I stated that some of the staff were beginning to make plans for my retirement get-together, and that it would be nice for everyone to be included; and hopefully, that she and I could have a reconciliation before then. I also indicated I had some laundered outreach clothing I would like to drop off at the VET Center that staff members might like to have since I don't need them anymore. Ms. Fortin then replied she was not comfortable with this and preferred I meet someone away from the VET Center to give them these items. I told her that would be fine if that was better for her. Overall, I felt good that Ms. Fortin had called and thought this was a positive step in the right direction.

- **February 23, 2018:** I received an email from Dale Willis reiterating that I was not to go to the VET Center without calling him first, which was based on Ms. Fortin not being comfortable with me there due to reasons that were never explained to me. He further stated if I showed up at the VET Center the police would be called. He mentioned he made this determination because of being "very concerned about some staff and the anxiety this situation has created."

- **February 23, 2018:** I responded to Dale's email because I wanted to know where all this was coming from, especially since I knew there was no rational basis for this.

- **February 23, 2018:** I forwarded these emails to members of the staff to make them aware of this exchange.

- **February 23, 2018:** A colleague responded to me via email and concurred all of this was an overreaction. She agreed with my reasons for why this was happening. My colleague further said she felt angry for me, and that those responsible for this was the real threat, not me.

- **February 27, 2018:** I received an email from Dale Willis (District 1 Deputy Director) telling me he received additionally information which made him write his February 23rd email. He said it was his understanding that I pressured Ms. Fortin in the conversation she and I had on February 22nd by insisting on coming to the VET

Center, which I did not. He also said someone told him I had brought a gun into the VET Center within the past year, and that if it is true or not this was the reason his tone had changed in his previous email. [The reference to the gun was hearsay. If this really happened, then why was it being brought up now and not a year ago when this supposedly occurred]

- **March 1, 2018:** I sent an email to Dale and everyone on the VET Center staff in response to his February 27th email in order to address my concerns and the inappropriate way this whole situation had been handled. I still felt Ms. Fortin was trying to isolate me from everyone for reasons mentioned previously. I expressed that I was being isolated and punished unfairly by this negative treatment, and how this was unwarranted since I had not done anything to deserve this treatment. I also pointed out how this situation deteriorated in my absence, and therefore, it was irrational to imply that I was somehow responsible for it. I indicated I wanted everyone to know where I actually stood, in order to help alleviate any fears or concerns that were lingering due to deceptive rumors.

- **March 1, 2018:** I received an email from a staff member who said she was "Sorry to see all this is happening to me." She also commented it was "Ridiculous" and "insane."

- **March 5, 2018:** I filed a grievance with the VA Office of Inspector General (OIG) stating the Readjustment Counseling Service (RCS), which is part of the Veterans Health Administration (VHA), had been engaged in unfair and unethical practices involving excessive clinical visit count expectations which had adversely impacted the health and well-being of counselors and degraded their ability to provide quality care to veterans and their families.

- **Mid-March 2018:** I met with John Kiernan at Senator Reed's Cranston, RI, office to address the harmful impact that the VET Center program's clinical productivity mandates were having on quality care and counselor welfare. I provided him with supporting documentation which substantiated my allegations.

- **March 31, 2018:** I had a Submassive Pulmonary Saddle Embolism that landed me in the ICU for 4 days at the Providence VA Medical Center and RI Hospital. I was told by doctors and nurses this was extremely serious and that people who have this type of embolism usually do not survive. A blood test revealed I do not have any hereditary risk factors for clotting. It was determined the embolism was a result of my sedentary activity during February and March, a consequence of the severe depression triggered by the unjust and discriminatory treatment I had received over the last two months from VET Center program management, leaving me feeling extremely hurt, angry, invalidated, betrayed, worthless, and hopeless.

- **April 4, 2018:** WPRI TV Channel 12 in Providence, RI aired my interview about the negative impact of the clinical productivity mandates in the VET Center program. (*https://www.wpri.com/news/combat-veteran-counselor-files-complaint-over-quota/*)

- **May 9, 2018:** NPR broadcast my interview regarding counselor burnout in the VET Center program. (*https://www.npr.org/2018/05/09/609653871/veterans-counselors-feeling-overworked?live=1*)

- **May 24, 2018:** Informal ORM EEO Mediation took place in Providence, RI to address my complaint. Nothing was resolved.

- **June 2018:** I connected with Jackie Garrick, the founder and CEO of Whistleblowers of America (WoA). She mentors whistleblowers through her organization and has a certification program for peer-to-peer support. She has been very supportive throughout my whistleblowing process.

- **June 2018:** Formal ORM EEO Mediation Process begins. Agency decision was unfavorably rendered on 02/05/2019.

- **June 9, 2018:** My mother died.

- **June 21, 2018:** *Military Times* published an article from my interview about VA leadership causing counselor burnout in the VET Center program. (*https://www.militarytimes.com/news/your-military/2018/06/21/crisis-in-counseling-how-va-leadership-is-driving-combat-veteran-counselors-to-burnout/*)

- **July 2018:** I attended a week-long Therapeutic Intensive while fasting with Michael Reddy in Pottstown, PA, involving Shamanism, Emotional Freedom Techniques (EFT), Dream Work, and Family Constellations. This significantly intensive therapeutic experience fostered my spiritual and emotional healing from the trauma I experienced due to the whistleblower retaliation against me by VA management. It helped me build resilience and allowed me to continue with my advocacy campaign to protect quality care and counselor welfare in the VET Center program.

- **August 21, 2018:** Senators Reed (D-RI) & Tester (D-MT) sent a joint letter to the Government Accountability Office (GAO) requesting an investigation into my allegations.

- **Oct 1, 2018:** WPRI TV Channel 12 in Providence, RI, aired my interview regarding VA management's whistleblower retaliation against me. (*https://www.wpri.com/target-12/feds-move-forward-on-ri-whistleblower-s-claim-of-harassment-hostility/*)

- **January – June 2019:** I participated in the "*School of Awakening*" with Eckhart Tolle which involved two live retreats, monthly online sessions, readings, videos, and meditation. This further enhanced my healing process and strengthened my resilience.

- **March 2019:** I attended an annual Traditional Chinese Medicine & Qi Gong Conference in Washington, DC where I met Qi Gong Grand Master Effie Chow.

- **May 30, 2019:** I had a day-long interview with an NBC crew at my home in Smithfield, RI. This involved hours of recorded interviews and verified the authenticity of my supporting documents.

- **Mid-June 2019:** I attended a 9-day Qi Gong program in San Francisco, CA, facilitated by Dr. Effie Chow. This was also very beneficial in contributing to my healing success.

- **July 14, 2019:** I was present at the Veterans Community Conversation event at Slater Memorial Park in Pawtucket, RI. Here I spoke with Senator Reed about the VET Center program issues I had raised, as well as with Congressman Cicilline, who sponsored the gathering. I also had a conversation about these concerns with Congressman Takano (D-CA), who is the Chairman of the House Veterans Affairs Committee.

- **July 23,2019:** My Statement for the Record regarding VA VET Center program issues was submitted to the House Veterans Affairs Oversight & Investigations Subcommittee by Jackie Garrick, CEO of Whistleblowers of America, where she presented her testimony regarding my case in person before the committee.

- **End of July 2019:** I attended the National Whistleblowers Summit in Washington, DC. During this trip, on July 31st I had an appointment at Senator Reed's office with John Nobrega to discuss the VET Center program issues. I provided him with documentation to substantiate my allegations. Concurrently, NBC Pentagon Correspondent, Courtney Kube, interviewed me with a camera crew outside of Senator Reed's office prior to my meeting.

- **Nov 3, 2019:** NBC aired my interview about the harmful effect VA leadership's clinical productivity policies were having on mental health care for veterans in the VET Center program. (*https://www. nbcnews.com/health/health-care/former-therapist-va-hurting-mental-health-care-combat-veterans-its-n1075781*)

- **Nov 10, 2019:** The NBC Today Show broadcast my interview regarding the VET Center program.(*https://www.today.com/*

video/successful-program-for-veterans-with-ptsd-is-being-threatened-73234501561)

- **November 13, 2019:** I had a meeting with Chris Bizzacco at Congressman Cicilline's Pawtucket, RI, office. We discussed the compromised quality care and counselor burnout issues in the VET Center program. I gave him documentation to validate these allegations.

- **November 2019:** The Government Accountability Office (GAO) commenced their investigation into these claims.

- **November 2019:** I participated in a *Conscious Manifestation* Program with Eckhart Tolle as part of my spiritual and emotional self-care.

- **Nov 24, 2019:** Rhode Island Cable PEG TV, Veterans Information Network, interviewed me about quality care for veterans being threatened in the VA's VET Center program. This interview aired multiple times the following month in Rhode Island. (*https://www. youtube.com/PEG TV/VA-VET Center Program Quality Care Being Compromised*)

- **Jan 9, 2020:** WPRI TV Channel 12 in Providence, RI, broadcast my interview regarding the ongoing federal GAO investigation into my allegations about the harmful counselor productivity expectations in the VET Center program. (*https://www.wpri.com/ target-12/feds-investigate-combat-vet-counselor-quota-claim/*)

- **March 10, 2020:** I was interviewed by the GAO lead investigator, Malissa Winograd, and her team as part of their investigation.

- **September 23, 2020:** The GAO released their report on the investigation which validated my claims.

- **Sep 28, 2020:** *Military Times* published an article from my interview with them regarding the need to rectify counselor burnout in the VET Center program. (*https://www.militarytimes.com/news/your-military/2020/09/28/ report-vet-counseling-fixes-needed-to-fight-counselor-burnout/*)

- **September 30, 2020:** I addressed my concerns about the VA's response to the GAO report via email, teleconference, and Zoom separately with Congressman Cicilline and Senator Reed's staff, the GAO lead investigator (Malissa Winograd), and the media (i.e., NBC, NPR, etc.).

- **Oct 5, 2020:** WPRI TV Channel 12 in Providence, RI, aired my interview about the GAO validating my claims regarding the detrimental productivity expectations forced on counselors in the VET Center program. (*https://www.wpri.com/target-12/feds-back-smithfield-whistleblowers-claim-of-stressful-counseling-quotas/*)

- **October 2020:** I phoned and sent emails to the major national-level Veteran Service Organizations in Washington, DC, to solicit support for corrective action in the VET Center program.

- **December 2020:** I was informed by John Nobrega at Senator Reed's office about the VET Center Improvement Act legislation that was initiated and drafted by Senator Reed (D-RI) and Senator Tester (D-MT), based on the GAO's findings from their inquiry and my documentation.

- **January 2021:** I provided feedback and suggested language to John Nobrega at Senator Reed's office for some parts of the VET Center Improvement Act which was incorporated into the Bill (S. 1944).

- **March 2021:** The No Trespass incident occurred at the Warwick, RI, VET Center.

- **April 1, 2021:** I hired a law firm to get the No Trespass Order rescinded (Pannone, Lopes, Devereaux & O'Gara LLC in Johnston, RI).

- **April 12, 2021:** I gave a presentation at the Rhode Island College (RIC) School of Social Work (SSW) for one of my former professor's classes about my whistleblowing crusade and the retaliation I experienced.

- **April-May 2021:** I was a guest speaker at numerous Veteran Service Organizations' monthly meetings in Rhode Island to raise awareness about the quality of care and counselor burnout issues in the VA VET Center program, and included the retaliation tactics used against me and others who spoke up about these concerns (e.g., Military Order of Foreign Wars (MOFW), Paralyzed Veterans of America (PVA) in Washington DC via Zoom, United Veterans Council (UVC) which is comprised of VSO state commanders, and the House Veterans Advisor Council (HVAC)).

- **May 10, 2021:** I participated in Congressman Cicilline's Veteran Advisory Board Zoom meeting where I explained the issues concerning quality care and counselor burnout in the VET Center program. I thanked the Congressman for supporting the VET Center Improvement Act. In turn, he thanked me for my advocacy efforts which made this legislation possible.

- **May 15, 2021:** I attended the Vietnam Veteran Wall dedication at Veteran Memorial Park in Fall River, MA. I spoke with Congressmen Keating (D-MA) and Auchincloss (D-MA) after the ceremony about issues in the VET Center program and the VET Center Improvement Act.

- **Jun 28, 2021:** The No Trespass Order was revoked.

- **Sep 20, 2021:** My attorney sent a letter to Ms. Rochelle Fortin, director at the Warwick, RI, VET Center and Mike Fisher, RCS Chief Officer, warning them that any further defamation of character or retaliation directed at me would result in legal action being taken against them and the VA.

- **Oct 20, 2021:** Rhode Island Cable PEG TV, Veterans Information Network, interviewed me about the legislation that was introduced to the U.S. Congress to resolve compromised quality care and counselor burnout issues in the VET Center program. The interview aired multiple times in Rhode Island the following month. (*https://drive. google.com/file/d/1Z3m-k_NH0AFH7QkSP7XESCbVg1CrIUT0/ view?usp=sharing*)

- **Nov 23, 2021:** WPRI TV Channel 12 in Providence, RI, broadcast my interview regarding the congressional legislation that was introduced to the House and Senate Committees on Veterans Affairs, as a result of the GAO investigation which substantiated my allegations about compromised quality care and counselor burnout in the VA's VET Center program. (*https://www.wpri.com/military/ ri-whistleblower-prompts-congress-to-consider-more-oversight-of-va/*)

- **Jan 27, 2022:** The *Valley Breeze* (Rhode Island Magazine) published an article from my interview regarding the VET Center issues I addressed with federal authorities, including the GoFundMe site which was established on my behalf by Whistleblowers of America (WoA) to recoup the legal expenses I had accumulated due to the retaliation perpetrated against me by VA management [*https://gofund.me/8573b27f*]. (*https://www.valleybreeze.com/news/ smithfields-blickwedel-seeks-help-after-whistleblower-retaliation/ article_804436ca-7da1-11ec-a2ff-8bc51714022dhtml*)

The authors are available for speaking engagements and book clubs. They can be contacted individually at:

Ted Blickwedel: *ted.blickwedel2@verizon.net*
Jerome R. Strayve, Jr.: *info@jrstrayvejr.com*

ACKNOWLEDGEMENTS

I first want to thank my wife, Julie, for her patience, loving and stead-fast support which helped me to successfully complete this project and get through the traumatic challenges I faced that were the impetus behind writing this book.

I would like to especially recognize my colleagues in the VA VET Center Program across the country for their courage in backing me throughout my whistleblowing ordeal. Their consultation, assistance and encouragement were crucial in numerous ways which validated my efforts and helped me to press on with my advocacy crusade and the writing of *Broken Promises*.

I also must extend my deepest appreciation to all the individuals who were interviewed for this book. This provided significant per-spectives from VET Center directors, counselors and clients, as well as whistleblower advocates who confirmed the issues addressed in *Broken Promises* and the need for constructive change in the Veterans Health Administration to protect quality care for veterans and the welfare of counselors who serve them.

Additionally, a big expression of gratitude goes out to my healing and spiritual mentors, peers, relatives and friends who compassion-ately stood by me in my most difficult moments, which enhanced my resilience and further inspired me to continue surging forward to *speak truth to power*.

I, too, thank Senator Jack Reed, Senator Jon Tester, Congressman David Cicilline and their team for their initiation and sponsorship of the ***VET Center Improvement Act*** which was introduced to the House and Senate Veterans Affairs Committees to hold the VA accountable for safeguarding quality care and the well-being of their clinical staff.

My co-author and I would like to thank our content editor, Trisha Gooch, for her kind yet disciplined contribution to *Broken Promises*. Our "Steel Magnolia's" contribution to ensuring we effectively communicated my story has proven invaluable. We would also like to thank Tamara Merrill, Craig McCleod, Elle Ravenswood, Thomas Courtney and Gerald Buckley for their assistance during the writing process.

Again, Tamara Merrill for her technical support and Adam Houge for his multi-faceted contributions.

I would also like to thank my friend, colleague, co-author and fellow Marine, Jerome R. Strayve, Jr. Jerry and I have spent the better part of a year weaving my story into this heart-felt book. I have learned so much working with him. His passion for my venture and our friendship have grown transforming my journey into this amazing expose. Without him, my story would never have been written. Thank you, Jerry.

Finally, I am grateful for everyone who has been donating to the GoFundMe site established on my behalf so I can recoup the legal fees I have accumulated to defend myself against the retaliation I've endured from VA management (*https://gofund.me/8573b27f*).

ABOUT THE AUTHORS

TED BLICKWEDEL is a retired Marine Corps Lieutenant Colonel and combat veteran who became a Licensed Clinical Social Worker after he retired from the military. He worked as a counselor at the VA VET Center in Warwick, RI, from 2009 to 2018 where he provided mental health care for fellow veterans. In 2017, during his tenure at the VET Center, he began to *speak truth to power* in an effort to have VA VET Center Management revise their clinical productivity policies that were harmful to counselors and compromising quality care for veterans. His subsequent whistleblowing campaign came at great price, personally, professionally, financially, and health wise. He is currently urging the United States Congress to pass legislation that has been introduced to the House and Senate Veterans Affairs Committees, as a result of a federal GAO investigation he helped instigate which substantiated his allegations. This legislation will protect the quality of services to our veterans and their families, as well as safeguard the welfare of counselors who care for them at over 300 VET Centers nationwide. Blickwedel's crusade to rectify compromised mental health care and counselor well-being within the VA VET Center program has been featured on NBC and NPR, to include the *Military Times*, other publications and local news broadcasts.

JEROME R STRAYVE JR served with Ted Blickwedel when both were young lieutenants in the Marine Corps. Forty years later their paths crossed again. This led the two of them to co-author Blickwedel's story in *Broken Promises*.

Strayve was born to a nomadic military family, attending nine schools before entering college. Following service in the United States Marine Corps, he raised a family while working as a financial representative and serial entrepreneur. Raising his young children, he discovered his talent for *spinning tales*, regaling them with spontaneous bedtime stories.

Soon his passion for history spoke to him and he jumped into writing. His fiction works include the first two books in a four-book series, *Braxton's Century*. Book three in the series will be published in February 2023. He published *First Spouse of The United States* in 2019 and is releasing the sequel, *POTUS DOWN*, in the fall of 2022. Learn more about JR STRAYVE JR at *www.jrstravyejr.com*.

OTHER BOOKS BY JEROME R. STRAYVE, JR.

Strayve uses the pen name, **JR STRAYVE JR** when writing fiction.

BRAXTON'S CENTURY Vol 1

"A riveting escapist fantasy I couldn't put down."

Red, white, and orange light fiendishly dances within Aurelio Palace's soaring glass dome. The midnight sky of England's rolling countryside has been set aglow. It is 1870.

The palace has been set on fire by the ten year old Prince Braxton, third son of the fictional Prince and Princess of Wales.

Intense heat soaring up into the glittering dome, loosens the lead securing the glass panes to the massive onion shaped dome's latticework.

The panes shift then plummet down to the rotunda's glittering marble floor, exploding in all directions, a million knife-like shards sure to dissect all within their murderous path.

This is the first of many bizarre but calculated turns of events Braxton sets in motion during this 19th century alternative historical epic.

Readers that enjoy exotic travel, magical settings, beautiful women, handsome men, brilliant dialogue, action, adventures, twists and turns, and fluid sexuality are sure to be seduced by Braxton as he comes of age.

Buckle up and dive into this saga, journeying alongside Braxton tearing through life on his own terms, crafting history's greatest hundred years.

Amazon: *https://www.amazon.com/J-R-Strayve-Jr/e/B08SHQ78CD*

BRAXTON'S CENTURY Vol 2

When Prince Braxton departs Vienna in the 1880s, following a night of debauchery dressed in gold as the ancient God of War, Mars. He leaves behind a tangle of threats, promises, and compromised nobles, his trading empire intact. Or is it?

Braxton's larger-than-life wheeling and dealings take him from Russia to Japan, Hong Kong, and India. But his obsessions are sucking every ounce of Braxton's being from within.

Continue your journey through history's most dynamic century as Prince Braxton tears through life on his own terms. When life forces him to decide his path, what—and who—will he choose?

This second volume of four scorches a trail spanning from 1880 to 1884. The entire saga features a century of world wars and engineering marvels that one might recognize with requited and unrequited love, romances that defy social mores, death, revolutions, and espionage that casts this tale into one that could have been had Prince Braxton been real.

Available on Amazon: *https://www.amazon.com/dp/B08YNH7KWX*

BRAXTON'S CENTURY Vol 3

Join Braxton as the Europe jumps into the Roaring '20s and then plumets into a worldwide depression drawing the continent closer to war.

Available Early 2023

BRAXTON'S CENTURY Vol 4

WW II changes the global geopolitical landscape. Braxton's Century comes to a close as Braxton sets the stage for characters larger than life destined to emerge in the trilogy, Millennial Moguls Unhinged!

Available Late 2023

FIRST SPOUSE OF THE UNITED STATES

First Spouse of the United States: Star Athlete & War Hero Battles Societal Boundaries and Washington Elite parallels today's political and social unrest.

Politically controversial and pragmatic, witness an unlikely duo in their quest for the White House. Watch both Democrats and Republicans facilitated by a complicit media, maneuver to eat their own.

Available on Amazon: *https://amzn.com/B07PNS1FD6*

POTUS DOWN

(Sequel to First Spouse Of The United States)

Available Fall 2022

THE LIEUTENANT & THE VINTER
(A Short Story)

German SS Lt. Georg von Reichenau, recently recovering from wounds sustained in battle has been assigned to French Burgundy. Andre Beaulieu, a gold medal winning Olympian down-hill racer is working to maintain his family's vineyard during the WWII German occupation. The Lieutenant remembers Andre. Andre has no recollection of how they met, for he lives with a different memory of a woman he cannot forget or find.

Adult Content.

Available on Amazon: *https://amzn.com/B08F9N7GW7*

VAINGLORIOUS

Prequel to the Braxton Century Series Set in the fabulously glittering court of the early 1830s, Russian Grand Duchess navigates the treacherous gauntlet thwarting the powerful men attempting to control Her.

… she has no choice but to obey the czar, her father's every command or she, too, would become "forever indisposed," as had her mother. If you think Henry VIII was tyrannical … read this novella.

The czar's court is as villainous as is he. Ekaterina violently opposes the marriage and ultimately surrenders to her father, the czar's, politically motivated marriage betrothal. Her future husband, Prince Gregor, handsome and sexually attractive, is not her prince charming. His wedding gift to her is blatant womanizing and ceaseless conniving to steal power and prestige, planting the seeds for the contempt and disdain further fueling her hatred for him.

Through the years, even the czar comes to share Ekaterina's hatred for Prince Gregor. The saying, "misery makes for strange bedfellows," draws the czar and Ekaterina together in a devious plan of imperial proportions to rid themselves of Gregor. A plan that would succeed beyond their wildest nightmare.

Author JR Strayve, Jr is a master storyteller, adept at weaving fact and fiction together in a seamless, jaw-dropping tale of Ekaterina's determination to rule her own life amidst Russian political intrigue and savagery.

Join Ekaterina in her story, A prequel to Braxton's Century Volume I. Readers are further mesmerized by the young Grand Duchess Ekaterina, fully understanding why she is later so closely drawn to Prince Braxton, becoming his confidante and benefactor.

Available: https://books2read.com/u/3n7k15

JR STRAYVE JR IS AVAILABLE FOR SPEAKING ENGAGEMENTS
AT BOOK CLUBS & PROFESSIONAL GROUPS.
Please forward inquiries to: *info@jrstrayvejr.com*

**If you would like to keep abreast of the author's
upcoming projects, go to**
WWW.JRSTRAYVEJR.COM
and subscribe to his newsletter